brilliant

agile project
management

agile project management

A practical guide to using Agile, Scrum and Kanban

Rob Cole and Edward Scotcher

PEARSON

Harlow, England • London • New York • Boston • San Francisco • Toronto • Sydney • Auckland • Singapore • Hong Kong
Tokyo • Seoul • Taipei • New Delhi • Cape Town • São Paulo • Mexico City • Madrid • Amsterdam • Munich • Paris • Milan

Pearson Education Limited
Edinburgh Gate
Harlow CM20 2JE
United Kingdom
Tel: +44 (0)1279 623623
Web: www.pearson.com/uk

First published 2015 (print and electronic)

ISBN: 978–1–292–06356–0 (print)
       978–1–292–06358–4 (PDF)
       978–1–292–06357–7 (eText)
       978–1–292–06359–1 (ePub)

British Library Cataloguing-in-Publication Data
Cole, Rob, author.
  Brilliant Agile project management : a practical guide to using Agile, Scrum and Kanban / Rob Cole and Edward Scotcher.
    pages cm.—(Brillian)
  Includes index.
  ISBN 978-1-292-06356-0 (pbk.)
  1. Agile software development.   2. Scrum (Computer software development)
  3. Just-in-time systems. 4. Computer software—Development.   5. Information technology projects—Management.   I. Scotcher, Edward, author.   II. Title.
  QA76.76.D47C6434 2015
  005.1--dc23
                         2015034100

10 9 8 7 6 5 4 3
19 18

Cartoons by Ken Pyne

Print edition typeset in 10 pts Plantin MT Pro by 76
Print edition printed in Great Britain by Ashford Colour Press Ltd.

NOTE THAT ANY PAGE CROSS REFERENCES REFER TO THE PRINT EDITION

For Alfie and Cissie, Ella and Alice

For Nkeiru, Lisa, Amara and Joe

Contents

About the authors

Rob Cole is a project management consultant with over 20 years of experience. He specialises in project troubleshooting and mentoring. Rob has been involved in the Agile community from its earliest days and is a practising Scrum Master.

Rob can be contacted at: **robacole@btopenworld.com**

Edward Scotcher is a leading agile product manager, project manager, trainer and coach. He specialises in helping organisations, teams and individuals adopt Agile in a practical and sustainable way.

Ed can be contacted at: **edward.scotcher@agilityinmind.co.uk**

CHAPTER 1

A brave new world: introducing *agile*

Introduction

Agile project management is centre stage at the moment and quite rightly so. Missions, ventures or whatever else *projects* are dubbed have been around from the year dot and have been going wrong for just as long. Now a *so-called* new kid on the block has come along promising to change all that and for once it's not hype. Seasoned veterans think they've seen it all before with other project management frameworks but this time it's very different. There's a revolution going on.

Chances are you've already heard quite a bit about the *world of agile*. There's no multi-million pound marketing campaign behind the good press and it's nearly all down to word of mouth. At times it might seem like everyone has either already signed up or is going down that route in the very near future. But in reality there are plenty of people and organisations still pondering their first move.

Brilliant Agile Project Management provides an insight into that brave new world with enough to help you make informed decisions about what will and will not work for you. This isn't a massive tome and that's intentional. But in true *agile* fashion it contains enough to start heading off in the right direction and contains the minimum you need to know to get the maximum return.

 All that is gold does not glitter. Not all those who wander are lost.

J.R.R. Tolkien

Agile beginnings

Despite an exponential growth of interest in all things *agile* and unprecedented levels of adoption recently, this isn't an overnight success story. The roots go back *at least* 20 years and the birth occurred against a backdrop of widespread frustration at regular project failure. The *agile* journey is a pretty interesting tale but it's only of academic who-did-what-and-when interest to us. The main thing is that along the way there was a quiet peoples' revolution.

And in a world where there is nothing new under the sun, *agile project management* is different, *very different.*

At first glance everything looks very similar in both the old and new worlds. Just as always, there are projects with goals, budgets, timescales and multiple problems along the way to delivery. It's only when you sneak a peek under the bonnet that the differences start to become clear. The end destination may be pretty much the same but there's a world of difference in *how* to get there. More importantly, if you play your cards right there's a better chance than ever of arriving with a satisfied smile and a wallet intact.

Contrary to recent publicity, even before *agile* came along projects were delivered successfully. Quite a few were even delivered on time and within budget to happy business teams – best to whisper that quietly in certain *agile* circles! However, in spite of the successes, far too many were late or over budget or even worse they didn't deliver what the business wanted in the first place. With *agile* the odds of a positive outcome are much higher.

It doesn't mean that *agile* projects don't occasionally go off track. To absolutely guarantee success you need a genie and a lamp. But with *agile* the days of long-running, huge scale multi-million pound failures are long gone. Also gone is the risk of getting in so deep that the only option is throwing good money after bad. When things go off-piste with *agile* it happens quickly and there's plenty of time to learn lessons and recover.

 **example**

As part of bringing in a programme to introduce e-services, a large government organisation embarked on an expensive build of its technical infrastructure as well. As part of delivering the first multi-million pound offering it was deemed necessary to invest even more millions on new computing firepower that could support the whole extensive shooting match. This long-term investment was made even though the first delivery was nothing more than an electronic version of a form requiring just minutes to complete in the old days.

Several setbacks later the big day came and cyber corks were popping all around the high-tech nerve centre for the development. The huge cost was forgotten as the management team celebrated with the army of consultants working on the project. Backs were slapped and arrangements were made to relocate to the nearest pub for a real party. But as the first drinks were sipped, nobody was actually using the new system – and that wasn't considered to be a big issue.

State of the art equipment. A high-tech alternative to filling in a form. No one using the new system. No business value delivered yet. The journey and the beauty of the delivery were being celebrated. Nobody seemed to care whether the new system was actually being used.

The *Agile Manifesto*

Agile goes way back and most consider Lean techniques as used within the automotive industry to be the birthplace of the modern *agile* movement. The early charge was into Information

Technology (IT) where it wasn't unusual for projects costing millions to abort with little or nothing tangible being delivered. The pace really started to crank up in 2001 – a watershed year for the *agile* movement.

In February 2001, 17 independent practitioners met at the Snowbird resort in Utah to discuss software development methods and they published the *Manifesto for Agile Software Development*. Apparently the participants didn't agree about much but they found consensus around four key values. To this day their statement remains a foundation stone for the *agile* movement.

Manifesto for Agile Software Development

We are uncovering better ways of developing software by doing it and helping others do it. Through this work we have come to value:

Individuals and interactions *over processes and tools*

Working software over comprehensive documentation

Customer collaboration over contract negotiation

Responding to change *over following a plan*

That is, while there is value in the items on the right, we value the items on the left more.

©Agile Manifesto Copyright 2001: Kent Beck, Mike Beedle, Arie van Bennekum, Alistair Cockburn, Ward Cunningham, Martin Fowler, James Grenning, Jim Highsmith, Andrew Hunt, Ron Jeffries, Jon Kern, Brian Marick, Robert C. Martin, Steve Mellor, Ken Schwaber, Jeff Sutherland, Dave Thomas. This declaration may be freely copied in any form, but only in its entirety through this notice.

If you don't work in the IT mega-industry alarm bells might be ringing at the mention of *working software*. One of the recurring questions is whether *agile* only works well in the software development business or whether it can be applied more widely. Admittedly the *Agile Manifesto* was born of a desire to improve software delivery but the principles can be universally applied. Just substitute *working products* for *working software* in the manifesto as a case in point.

The Manifesto is supplemented by *Principles Behind the Agile Manifesto*. Once again, it's easy to remove the software-centric emphasis. The key is to understand the philosophy underpinning the principles.

Principles Behind the Agile Manifesto

We follow these principles:

✔ Our highest priority is to satisfy the customer through early and continuous delivery of valuable software.

✔ Welcome changing requirements, even late in development. Agile processes harness change for the customer's competitive advantage.

✔ Deliver working software frequently, from a couple of weeks to a couple of months, with a preference to the shorter timescale.

✔ Business people and developers must work together daily throughout the project.

✔ Build projects around motivated individuals. Give them the environment and support they need, and trust them to get the job done.

✔ The most efficient and effective method of conveying information to and within a development team is face-to-face conversation.

✔ Working software is the primary measure of progress.

✔ Agile processes promote sustainable development. The sponsors, developers, and users should be able to maintain a constant pace indefinitely.

✔ Continuous attention to technical excellence and good design enhances agility.

▶

✔ Simplicity – the art of maximizing the amount of work not done is essential.

✔ The best architectures, requirements, and designs emerge from self-organizing teams.

✔ At regular intervals, the team reflects on how to become more effective, then tunes and adjusts its behaviour accordingly.

©Agile Manifesto Copyright 2001: Kent Beck, Mike Beedle, Arie van Bennekum, Alistair Cockburn, Ward Cunningham, Martin Fowler, James Grenning, Jim Highsmith, Andrew Hunt, Ron Jeffries, Jon Kern, Brian Marick, Robert C. Martin, Steve Mellor, Ken Schwaber, Jeff Sutherland, Dave Thomas. This declaration may be freely copied in any form, but only in its entirety through this notice.

Finally, as an adjunct to the Manifesto, another bunch of heavy hitters produced the *Declaration of Interdependence*. It's less well-known and less frequently mentioned in dispatches but from a project management perspective this sums it up in a nutshell.

The Declaration of Interdependence

Agile and adaptive approaches for linking people, projects and value.

We are a community of project leaders that are highly successful at delivering results. To achieve these results:

✔ We **increase return on investment** by making continuous flow of value our focus.

✔ We **deliver reliable results** by engaging customers in frequent interactions and shared ownership.

✔ We **expect uncertainty** and manage for it through iterations, anticipation, and adaptation.

▶

✔ We **unleash creativity and innovation** by recognizing that individuals are the ultimate source of value, and creating an environment where they can make a difference.

✔ We **boost performance** through group accountability for results and shared responsibility for team effectiveness.

✔ We **improve effectiveness and reliability** through situationally specific strategies, processes and practices.

©2005 David Anderson, Sanjiv Augustine, Christopher Avery, Alistair Cockburn, Mike Cohn, Doug DeCarlo, Donna Fitzgerald, Jim Highsmith, Ole Jepsen, Lowell Lindstrom, Todd Little, Kent McDonald, Pollyanna Pixton, Preston Smith and Robert Wysocki.

One key reason why *agile* thinking is taking the business world by storm is because it wins hearts and minds quickly. *Agile* certainly has great word of mouth and presses all the right PR buttons too. The core messages are simple, powerful and extremely appealing:

- We **increase return on investment**.
- We **deliver reliable results**.
- We **expect uncertainty**.
- We **unleash creativity and innovation**.
- We **boost performance**.
- We **improve effectiveness and reliability**.

The state of the project nation

The advance press is excellent but what exactly is the core problem with project management today? What is *agile* trying to fix?

The bottom line is that projects *regularly take longer than expected, cost more than budgeted for* and *quite often fail to deliver what was asked for.* That heady cocktail has resulted in a loss of business confidence. Traditional project management thinking has always acknowledged the importance of *time, cost* and *scope* and together they're known in the game as the *Project Management Triangle.* But so many projects get lost in there that it's more like the *Bermuda Triangle.*

Figure 1.1 The project management triangle

Because of this rigid relationship, one side of the triangle cannot be changed without affecting the others. There are always consequences if the *scope, time* or *cost* parameters are adjusted. This happens frequently with projects when new requirements are added, timescales are reined in or budgets are slashed. Of course it never happens the other way round! Over the years project teams have battled with trying to keep the three constraints balanced, invariably a case of *Mission Impossible.*

Straight from the kick-off of any project, the bean counters are out in force checking for any signs of overspending or of lost time. Project managers are under this double spotlight right up until the final delivery is made when the focus shifts immediately from *how much* and *when* to: is it any damn good? Late deliveries and extra cost are soon forgotten if what's delivered is what the customer wanted. This is a nightmare to navigate.

In the *agile* world, life is fundamentally different. The focus from the beginning is on *delivering business value. Agile* puts the conventional early obsession with cost and timescales to one side and concentrates on what the business *wants* or, more specifically, what it *really needs*. No more aiming for perfection, leading to simple ideas getting morphed into tremendously complex and elegant solutions. No more runaway budgets. No more customer dissatisfaction.

brilliant tip

Customers don't want better project management. They want better product delivery. All the *agile* tools and techniques exist solely to that end. Use whatever techniques get the best results but don't get hung up on the methods themselves. The ends are much more important than the means.

Keep the customer satisfied

Projects never start with an intention to overegg the scope. One of the age-old challenges is seen as avoiding unnecessary gold plating and keeping the solution down to the minimum required to do the job adequately. However, in an attempt to be rigorous and thorough about pinning the scope right down there's a tendency for our customers to leave no stone unturned when asked: *what do you want?* This is unintentionally made worse when obsessing about getting the detail spot on, as if we're asking: *is there anything else?* It's akin to putting children in a toyshop and permitting them a wish list without any constraints.

Matters are made even worse when the customer thinks it's *now or never* and concludes that the only way to get a few nice useful bells and whistles is to demand them all up front and *insist* life is intolerable without the full package. This all leads to a crazy situation of non-essential requirements with an inflated budget and overlong timescales. In sharp contrast the first delivery with *agile* is aimed at being far more bare bones; just enough core

features to get going and no more. The implicit understanding is that this will be added to over time in a measured way to build towards a fully featured solution.

With *agile* there's no mad dash to get *everything* at the January sales. Instead, let's start with a solid foundation and build from there.

Sorry, no change thank you

Under the old order once every 'i' is dotted and every 't' is crossed there's a huge emphasis on preventing change, or at least closely controlling it. Many popular frameworks for running projects, such as *PRINCE2*, focus heavily on pinning down the requirements and then introducing rigorous change control. Change is considered bad news – even frowned upon – and if anything does sneak through, the business gets charged through the nose for it.

Getting this formula to work is always a struggle because a desire for change is inevitable on any project. As a general rule of thumb this approach is pretty fruitful when it's implemented with rigour and the changes are few and far between. But even then, there are usually a number of battles along the way. Regrettably, the likely outcome is just on the right side of average, with a customer who is not unhappy with the outcome but far from delighted.

Additionally, not every project is on a road going directly from A to B where exact requirements can be buttoned down and where change is nothing more than a minor distraction. Most start life as a fledgling idea that needs validating in the real world and building on. Sometimes it's necessary to change track or even occasionally go back to the drawing board. That's the natural order for the evolution of most business ideas and it doesn't help when the approach to developing projects is swimming against the tide.

Agile is different. *Agile* embraces change and even encourages it. Change is not seen as the enemy, it's seen as an important part of the evolution of any good idea. *Agile* works toward delivering the bare necessities in the shortest possible time to market, so they can be tested early. Evolution is a natural part of the process and change is no big deal. This is exactly what customers need in most situations and it's no wonder this is like a breath of fresh air to them.

Start small, cheap and quick

The intentions of the *Agile Manifesto*, principles and other elements of *agile* philosophy are great but how does this translate into action? How exactly is *agile* so different? Well, at the heart of the answer to this is that it starts off with a totally different approach to delivery and everything flows from there. Instead of beginning with a wish list as long as your arm and a restraining order on any change, *agile* begins by identifying the minimum needed to get going and builds from there. This is usually dubbed *the minimum viable product (MVP)* or the *minimum feature set (MFS)*.

In practice, both describe the same thing. Namely the smallest possible delivery that addresses the business needs, creates the desired customer experience, and can hence be marketed and sold successfully. This reduces the time to market, is cheaper and gets the job done adequately. It can therefore be delivered more quickly than a fat, feature-rich solution. Less is more.

---

brilliant example

Starting a new job straight out of school, college or university requires a little pre-planning before walking through the door on the big day. Especially if the new role is with a very conservative firm with high sartorial expectations.

Treated as *traditional* project this might lead to an extensive wish-list and a big-budget shopping spree:

- 3 suits (to be circulated)
- 10 shirts (to avoid a weekly wash)
- 5 ties (to provide choice)
- 2 pairs of shoes (one black, one brown)
- 1 overcoat (winter is only a 6 months away)
- 10 sets of underwear
- 1 car to get to the station (5 miles away)
- 1 bicycle in case the car breaks down (and waterproofs of course).

The purchasing could be done over a series of weekends – buying the suits might require a couple of weekends in their own right. This could be batched into three or four mini sprees and must allow for returns and changes of heart. A budget of £10k will cover all eventualities.

Building in contingency, best to get cracking two months before the start date. Oh dear, there's big trouble because the start date is next Monday. Better to execute a leaner, more *agile* plan: 1 suit, 2 shirts (wash and recycle in the first week), 2 ties (2-for-1 offer), a multipack of socks and pants. Use public transport or a taxi to the station.

Start with enough to get you going on Day 1. Don't forget, even some conventional firms have relaxed dress codes. Apologies for the male slant to this anecdote. Feel free to substitute other apparel!

Well frankly, going overboard *from the very start* happens all the time with projects in the real world. Going back to our last example, a more pragmatic and *agile* approach sees the wardrobe built up over time – delivered incrementally, as and when needed. An unexpected cold patch might raise the priority of a new overcoat and it may well turn out that the car and bicycle are unnecessary luxuries. Who knows, after a few months a well-deserved relaxing break to get away from it all might be in the budget instead?

Identifying the MVP or MFS is a strategy for getting a product or product feature to market and testing the solution. The core idea can be adapted to almost any situation, even a new job. The MVP in our example is a well-groomed professional on Day 1! Nothing more! The additional clothes and equipment are nothing more than nice-to-haves. By the time the first pay cheque lands, the *project* will be in profit. By then, if all is going well, informed choices can be made about additional *features*. If not, it's very easy to change course.

brilliant tip

> *Agile* is great at getting projects onto the right track early on. Spotting what's absolutely essential from the outset will prevent the waste of resources and curtail lost opportunities.

An *agile* mind-set

It's usually dangerous to generalise but there are certain mental attributes that are well suited to an *agile* lifestyle. All of the *agile* frameworks are team-based and place a significant emphasis on teamwork, cooperation, collaboration and being adaptable. Getting on well with others and being fleet of foot sums it up for us. Hermits and dictators aren't likely to be keen advocates.

Certain organisational cultures struggle to embrace and adopt *agile* thinking. That's not a criticism, just a fact of life. Ultimately it's down to individuals, and it's worth thinking about character traits and whether the whole ethos appeals. In that sense it's no different to other delivery frameworks such as *PRINCE2*; some are likely to float more boats than others. Anyone can try and adapt to an *agile* environment but some flourish. Certain personal traits help enormously:

- collaborative,
- committed,
- focused,
- open,
- respectful,
- courageous,
- honest.

These characteristics are sought after in any work colleague or *anyone* for that matter. A top rating in all of them identifies an asset for any team or project environment and the likelihood of taking to *agile* like a duck to water. Don't be too worried if the feedback indicates a mark of *could do better* because *agile* creates a supportive set-up that encourages these attributes.

Running the risk of generalising again, *agilists* are prone to being very passionate. Some are even considered to be a little too evangelical or dogmatic but that's more about being over-enthusiastic than anything sinister. It isn't a religious cult. Dipping into any of the *agile* forums can be a chastening experience at times, especially for a newbie, so don't be led to believe it's their way or the highway! *Agilists* don't bite but they do bark mighty loud sometimes.

Getting *agile*

It's impossible to legislate for all the possible combinations of *agile* start points for organisations and their individuals. Occasionally, there are situations where a strategic decision is made by the Top Bananas to break with the past and go gung-ho for the Promised Land; when the right people are empowered to *make it happen* armed with an open chequebook and a specialist coach on tap. Great news if this happens but it's a rare event.

A more typical scenario occurs when an organisation is dogged by failed projects and one or more people are convinced there *must* be a better way. Then the launch is accompanied by very little corporate buy-in *initially* and a minimal or non-existent budget. This is more likely to happen and allows us to think about the *minimum* prerequisites for any aspiring *agile* organisation. It's a chance to pin down the *critical success factors* that must be given special and continual attention to bring about success.

 **brilliant** definition

Critical success factors (CSFs) are those things that must be in place to ensure success. Those things that guarantee a *right result*.

CSFs for an *agile* project typically include:

- **An appropriate project**. Don't get stuck into the Number 1 priority mission critical project that's behind schedule before it even begins. Best to start with a small one, focusing on proving the *agile* process works and ironing out any kinks. There's plenty of time to ramp up once on a roll.
- **Suitable people**. Not only to participate on the project itself but also to oversee the *agile* transformation. As a minimum, assemble people with an *agile* mind-set and the

desire to make it happen. It's going to be a big team push and it will need a team effort.

- **Realistic expectations**. Be realistic especially in the short term. Expect immediate results but allow time for the benefits to filter through. Getting it right up front requires an investment and occasionally it can require a step back to make two steps forward. Set the bar at a reasonable height and build from there.

- **Adequate training**. *Agile* frameworks are easy to get to grips with and reading material on the web is a decent start. But factor training and mentoring into the plan. *Agile* coaches and mentors are geared up to dipping in and out of organisations – start with at least a day per week if the budget permits and if not then even one day a fortnight is better than nothing.

In the spirit of the occasion treat getting an *agile* project up and *delivering* to be part of the launch MVP. Pay attention to the CSFs. Choose the project wisely and surround yourself with the right people. There's no guaranteeing success but it's easy to skew the odds massively in your favour.

brilliant example

In the full flush of arrogant youth and desperate to learn to drive on the cheap it's tempting to buy a car and cut out the expense of driving lessons by teaching oneself. It's easy enough to find pals who have already passed their test who want to be chauffeured around, perhaps even offering a few throwaway words of advice. Given time and possibly a couple of driving test retakes this tactic can work. For most it's a false economy and eventually it dawns that more formal coaching is more effective.

Cutting out training and mentoring is a false economy. At worst it can be an accident waiting to happen.

Agile outcomes

If the CEO is en route to a board meeting and happens to drop by to ask for a couple of promotional sound bites – what's the bottom line? What can the board, senior management team, shareholders and fellow employees reasonably expect as outcomes? *Why bother?*

Put simply, if executed with a reasonably deft touch, *agile* will deliver immediately with:

- **Early delivery of the MVP or MFS**. Quick to market and early validation of the core concept. An end to playing the waiting game.
- **Fit-for-purpose deliveries**. Deliveries will 'do what it says on the tin', time after time. No more crossing fingers and hoping for the best.
- **Smaller initial investment**. Beginning with a reasonable budget and investing further on proof of success. An end to high-risk endeavours and betting the farm for no good reason.
- **All round flexibility**. The ability to adjust and adapt to changing circumstances. No more meltdowns and recriminations at the whiff of a change request.
- **Improved team performance**. A virtuous circle of happy, engaged team members leading to improved performance. There's nothing wrong with smiling faces!

Most importantly, this isn't about creating low expectations. From Day 1 expect to see evidence that the goods are being delivered. *Be reasonable* of course but expect all of the above immediately!

brilliant tip

Tap into the buzz around the launch of a new project by spreading the word up front. Let the key players know what to expect and how things are going to be different, especially when it's the first project

of its kind. A couple of hours spent explaining *agile* fundamentals
will improve understanding and promote acceptance.

*This is educational PR and serves a specific purpose in setting out
the project stall.*

Spoilt for choice

Looking at the big picture and making sweeping observations is
all very interesting but when it comes to running programmes
and projects it's time to get down to specifics and chose an *agile*
framework to work within. There are plenty of excellent options
but we want to stay very focused by sticking with our three
favourites.

1. Lean

Considered to be one of the grandparents of the modern *agile*
movement. Well worth checking out, especially by swotting up
on the *7 Lean Principles*. Excellent, thought provoking material
but we're not sitting on the fence and it's not our first choice for
running projects.

7 Lean Principles

1 Optimise the whole
2 Eliminate waste
3 Build quality in
4 Learn constantly
5 Deliver fast
6 Engage
7 Keep getting better

2. Scrum

This is the current darling of the *agile* world and is in the process of taking the business world by storm, rightfully so because this framework is a game changer. It's sparking changes in the way businesses think and deliver projects. It's the agent for a quiet revolution and our favourite framework by far – the real deal.

A great choice for projects of all shapes and sizes.

3. Kanban

Despite our almost sycophantic support for Scrum, Kanban is right up there in our books and has plenty to offer in *certain situations*. It's an excellent alternative to Scrum and very easy to implement. Occasionally misrepresented and oversimplified but there's more to Kanban than first appears.

Unbeatable at getting visibility of delivery in any environment.

Variants and other options

Of course, there are many other agile options, especially when the focus is on IT software development projects. Don't be surprised if you come across subtle variations on the agile themes, frameworks and organisations. At the framework level, interesting variants and combos are beginning to appear with Scrumban, SAFe and others. All thought-provoking stuff but we suggest sticking with the quality brands initially.

No-go areas for agile projects:

- shopping for a wedding
- carrying out open heart surgery
- building a space shuttle
- during childbirth
- playing at an Irish cèilidh.

Too good to be true

The positive press about *agile,* and in particular Scrum, is a double-edged sword. The advantage is that it isn't a hard sell. The downside is that the expectations are sky high. Management teams are tuning into the sound bites – quicker, cheaper, better – and forgetting that there's no such thing as a free lunch. Managing these expectations is a challenge but no big deal if handled with a deft touch. There's nothing wrong with building on internal enthusiasm and tapping into the excitement. Just don't over-egg it.

Expect to deal with doubters and detractors. Genuine uncertainty is natural with any significant new venture, as is a degree of outright opposition and undermining criticism. An element of PR is required but on the whole it's best to let *agile* speak for itself.

 'I worked half my life to be an overnight success, and still it took me by surprise.'

Jessica Savitch

The final word

New projects play a vital role in the development of any organisation and the failure rate at the moment is way too high. At times there's a shoulder-shrugging acceptance that it's the way of the world. Cash and other resources are getting wasted too often without anyone batting an eyelid. To add insult to injury, businesses opportunities are lost when reserves are squandered and the well runs dry.

It doesn't have to be that way. *Agile* offers an alternative approach that stops the rot and makes it much easier to deliver *real* value consistently.

Taking the first *agile* step isn't hard and there's plenty of support available when needed. This book will help kick-start the journey. It isn't intended as a definitive guide as that would be a near impossible task; it isn't *War and Peace*. However, it does contain everything you need to get going and plenty of pointers regarding where to go from there.

Let's go for it!

 brilliant recap

- Study the *Agile Manifesto* and check out the *7 Lean Principles*, as they're the foundation stone of everything *agile*.
- *Agile* is *very* different and needs a different mind-set to get the best results.
- Start small if possible and always focus on delivering business value.
- Expect results immediately but be *reasonable*.
- Here comes the cavalry... but don't believe *all* the hype!

CHAPTER 2

Agile is different

Introduction

Nothing stands still for very long and change is inevitable. That applies to all individuals, businesses and even societies. Being able to adjust and progress is much more than a nice-to-have; it's essential to survive. Dinosaurs were all-powerful and ruled the world for well over 100 million years but they failed to evolve and now that's how they're remembered. Despite their glory days, the term *dinosaur* is now widely used as a derogatory tag for failing to move on.

In the early part of the 20th century J. Lyons teashops and F.W. Woolworth stores were huge success stories and by the 1950s both were icons of British enterprise and household names. Yet both institutions are unknown by the younger generation and are merely fond memories of a bygone age for nanny and grandad – going from boom to bust in less than 50 years. In a changing world both failed to adjust and were considered to be corporate dinosaurs by the end.

In the 21st century it's getting even tougher. Businesses are powered by silicon and need to move at the speed of light. Customers, users and market demand can change within weeks. There's no time for slow burners anymore and five-year development plans are out of the question. Time to market is all-important and organisations must have the ability to change direction quickly; taking a fledgling idea from concept to cash almost overnight in order to stay relevant *and* solvent.

Conventional project management is struggling to adapt to this fast-moving new world because being *fleet of foot* doesn't come naturally. *Agile project management* is based on a totally different approach and copes perfectly. It's based on a mind-set that's tuned into the needs of contemporary businesses and provides exactly what's required to avoid going the same way as the dinosaurs.

brilliant example

Tesco has 40,000 product lines. It sells everything from car insurance to crisps. It also closes branches, lays off staff and issues profit warnings faster than awarding *Clubcard* points. Aldi, a newcomer in the UK market, has just 2,000 product lines. It's taking on staff, opening branches and making great profits. The question is whether Tesco is too big to adapt before Aldi takes its market share?

Businesses lose their way all the time. Losing focus or just getting out of shape is easy and the fall from grace can be rapid.

The darkest hours

The fast-moving pace of the modern business world has certainly brought matters to a head but organisations have been unhappy for a very long time with the deal they're getting from conventional project management. Projects regularly misfire and it's not unusual for project sponsors to feel trapped in a loveless marriage of convenience with no choice but to make the most out of a very bad situation. The business team ends up grumbling about 'that darn project' but usually just accept their fate with a shrug of their shoulders. Often, in final desperation, a shedload of money and other resource is thrown at a doomed mission to try and save the day. That hardly ever works out.

There's more bad news. The *established* ways of running projects are inclined to use rigid processes; setting out a plethora of rules to be followed, documents to write and meetings to go to. This usually comes with set phases to go through and planning alone can go on for weeks or months. Then each project stage operates in a world of its own, and adhering to the process is seen as more important than anything else. The end result of this is that the original *business intent* quite often gets lost along the way.

Finally, to make matters worse, the inmates regularly end up taking over the asylum and become a law unto themselves. Of course, project managers and their teams never set out with this as an objective, it just kind of happens. The imposition of rigorous processes and a tight control over *how* things get done often means that instead of the business directing projects, it's the other way round.

But the darkest hours are always just before the dawn. When projects are failing to deliver and businesses are struggling to survive, a *big* shake-up is needed. Going *agile* is that change agent.

 The measure of intelligence is the ability to change.

Albert Einstein

Agile fundamentals

Some people think *agile* is new. Others think it's something old but repackaged. Then there's the *it's just common sense* camp and those who say it doesn't work. You may even meet enthusiastic supporters who talk about it like it's some miracle cure for all business related problems. There are many different opinions and perspectives but the headline news is it's an incredible sea change in the approach to running projects with:

- people interacting face to face, solving their unique problems creatively;
- business involvement throughout the process from concept to cash;

- a reduced time to market to capture or retain competitive advantage;
- early initial deliveries and quick wins to get valuable feedback fast;
- fast incremental build of small enhancements to keep product fresh;
- flexibility and responsiveness to change built in to the very ethos;
- an ability to change focus to remain ahead of the game;
- the user's and customer's needs at the heart of decision making;
- *shipping the product is everything!*

---

brilliant example

A vital part of the *agile* philosophy is to ship early and frequently; to home in on the final solution by starting from the bare bones and adding steadily from there. The initial delivery is Lean and cost-effective. The core concepts are tested early with plenty of room for fine-tuning or outright changes in direction. This enables businesses to:

- start with essential requirements and no more;
- limit the starting investment to a minimum;
- predict the business benefits;
- empower the team;
- get cracking and build incrementally from there;
- change direction whenever necessary.

The litmus test for agile working practices is to make this vision a reality.

Agile demands we find a simpler approach to getting product shipped, putting people and the interactions between them at the centre of everything. The core tools and techniques are simple to use. Flexibility and change are an integral part of the package. Yes, the movement is steeped in common sense but that's no bad thing because the more complex something is the harder it is to master. If used wisely, *agile* will deliver better results than any prefabricated processes.

Agile ways of working put the focus more on visibility, transparency and interactions between people and less on dogmatic process. The ambition is to empower people, setting them free to concentrate on delivery. *Agile* frameworks provide a structure to operate within, not a step-by-step guide. It's frequently said that *agile* is easy to do and hard to do well. This is mainly because of the visibility, organisation and discipline it takes to make it work effectively.

There can be a feeling that *agile* ways of working are from the Wild West with little governance, no documentation, weak roles and ceremonies. But in fact that isn't the case at all. Everything is there but there's a significantly defter, more frequent touch, and *no process overload.*

 brilliant definition

At times there's a fine line between a *framework* and a *process*. In this context a framework is a series of flexible guidelines and a project process is typically far more strict and inflexible. One enables and the other constrains.

Auditing another way

Process overload is epitomised by the level of control and general interference normally imposed on projects. Many organisations get so hung up on *how* they do things that they've got far more worried about getting the process right than delivering results. This is especially true of large government bodies that are audited for their adherence to *PRINCE2*. This type of *procedural* review provides a way of testing how well the method is applied and where improvement may be beneficial. No reference is usually made to what the projects have delivered.

The mechanics of delivery are a secondary consideration for *agile* projects. The tools and techniques used are important of course but the guidance is far more flexible and can be moulded to suit the project *and* organisation. No two implementations of an *agile* framework are exactly identical although there will be remarkable similarities. There's no *agile* police and no auditing. Instead plenty of guidance and support is available and the spirit of the application is more important than the letter of the law. Important checks and balances are built into the core philosophy but *how* is considered less critical than *what*.

This unsettles anyone used to the *apparent* protection offered by the heavy processes associated with conventional projects. It needn't be, as *agile* projects are self-regulating in a far more transparent and effective way. *Agile* gets smaller-sized project chunks delivered quickly and this generates fast feedback on *actual working product*. Customers and end users always relate to this more than reviewing documentation because they can see it, use it and understand it. Early discovery of *the good, the bad and the ugly* is also a dream scenario, especially if any problems are highlighted – glitches are far easier to sort out when they're small and catching them early on reduces the risk of catastrophe late on in the game.

The *agile* alternative to auditing is less worried about adhering to a process and more concerned with protecting the end product.

---

brilliant example

Periodically there'd be a big flap at a large government agency when it was time for the annual *PRINCE2* audit. The project management office (PMO) would be panicking in search for any projects that adhered to the ▶

word; under normal conditions, adherence to *PRINCE2* was a little lax to say the least. Completing the audit successfully was considered quite an accolade but all that mattered to the project police was that *PRINCE2* was being followed, the closer the better.

What the projects delivered and whether they were successful was largely irrelevant.

Getting projects started

The time-to-market for any endeavour is crucial and the end-to-end period it takes to bring an idea to fruition includes more than the project duration itself. More often than not, getting to the launch pad involves significant effort up front and a lengthy gestation period is a big problem in its own right. Projects start life when the idea is first mooted and the clocks starts ticking straight away. Procrastination is a big problem and incredibly that's evolved into a process in its own right, called the *feasibility study*.

In fairness, one of the reasons why these pre-emptive assessments are normally considered necessary is because of the huge cost of projects. They're an attempt to work out up front whether ideas are viable and will generate an acceptable return on a sizeable investment – so that aspect of the investigation is sensible. However, feasibility studies are known for going off track and losing sight of the original intentions. They're notorious for political intrigue and pre-determined outcomes – the process is often about justifying a decision made up front, not about an independent assessment.

Agile cuts through all this, partly because launch costs are considerably reduced by focusing on the very early delivery of a piece of demonstrable product. Rather than spend money on thinking and assessing, far better to invest resource on trialling out the proposal. *Agile* makes it cheaper to test an idea for real and the conclusions are therefore more conclusive. Then the go/no-go assessment sits with the business and its decision is based on facts not conjecture.

It's better to try something and fail fast than to not try at all – so long as lessons are learned. Procrastination stifles progress and this can be compounded when the discussions, reviews, presentations and general arguments go on endlessly. Not doing something can cost more than getting on with it – especially in terms of demotivation. There's nothing worse than a winning idea getting knocked back for no good reason. Proving an idea works doesn't use up much of the budget and failure isn't *very* expensive either. Both offer more palatable and conclusive alternatives to daydreaming.

Once again *agile* turns tradition on its head and comes at the kick-off process in a totally different way. Every fledgling idea gets a crack of the whip and the bad 'uns are weeded out early on: with all decisions based on hard facts, not speculation.

brilliant example

In the early part of the new millennium a large government organisation had a specialist team dedicated to carrying out feasibility studies for potential new IT projects. All new ideas were supposed to be assessed for their return on investment. As funding was in short supply, only the ones with big returns were in with any chance.

The business team were too busy to be involved in these assessments and the IT reps drafted the recommendations based on their own interpretation of business thinking. This was well intentioned and driven by a desire by the IT team to be helpful, but the end result was that projects were commissioned for the wrong reasons. Sometimes it worked out OK and sometimes it didn't. It was a hit-and-miss affair.

It's bad enough when projects are executed badly. Even worse when they're kicked off for the wrong reasons.

Embracing change

Change is inevitable and it often happens fast. Change doesn't just come from inside the organisation either as pressures from a very savvy public, technological advancements and ever-changing attitudes mean that even the smallest failure to respond to change can mean losing the competitive edge in the market place. Conventional project processes put barriers in the way and penalises change. This is ultimately counterproductive and it's always going to be swimming against the tide. *Agile*, in contrast, encourages flexibility and facilitates change.

At the heart of everything *agile* is change. To become *agile* and stay that way will, in itself, demand change. Product development – in itself another facet of change – is made easier by working on fewer, smaller items at any given time. Big problems get broken down into smaller chunks so they're easier to understand, communicate and manage. Projects are encouraged to take baby steps because turning hundreds of tiny boats is a darn sight easier than turning an oil tanker. And anyone who gets to grips with that is truly *agile*.

Some interpret this inherent ability to respond to change as meaning that *agile* projects are plagued by last-minute, knee-jerk reactions. Admittedly this can be the case on any project and even with *agile* when it's done badly. But from the formative days, *Lean* manufacturing adopted the concept of making decisions *just in time (JIT)*. Without doubt, better decisions are made when they're based on fact rather than conjecture and it can take time for the detail to emerge. *Agile* encourages late *informed* decisions, made any time up to the point when failing to make a decision creates a problem in its own right. That just can't be handled by less nimble methods.

An easier life

This is all good news for the CEO, the board and the senior management team. It doesn't mean they can sit back and relax but it does allow them to concentrate more on the strategy rather than continually worrying about whether their projects are ever going to deliver. The high transparency of *agile* projects plus early and incremental delivery is a godsend to anyone at the top; it's a game changer in the relationship between senior execs and the projects they sponsor.

However, the biggest difference on going *agile* is reserved for the project team themselves. Job satisfaction is consistently better and the huge surge in *agile* popularity means that it's a great career move – there's nothing wrong with a bit of self-interest in this context! *Agile* also offers a better operating environment:

Clearer roles and responsibilities. This isn't about shirking or transferring responsibilities; it's about the *right* people making decisions. The business gets its say when it matters and ditto for the rest of the team.

Empowerment to take decisions. No more deferring to a higher authority that usually doesn't properly understand the context. Being in a position to make informed decisions like a responsible adult is both effective and liberating.

Power in the union. There is a sense of unity of purpose within *agile* teams and much less reliance on heroics. Individuals do shine of course but basking in glory is a collective thing. Looking after each other is part of the meal deal.

High energy and a positive vibe. The operating environment is upbeat, supportive, constructive and relaxed. This leads to team confidence in their collective ability to deliver and the feel-good factor is a big bonus.

Better results. Nobody wants to fail and being part of a successful team is much preferred *obviously*. Getting into a winning habit creates a confident mind-set. *Success breeds success.*

↗ brilliant impact

The most important reoccurring activity in an *agile* organisation is the removal of any blockers or constraints that are preventing the team from getting on with the job. These impediments to delivery can range from minor irritations to complex organisation handcuffs. They're productivity killers.

Being able to focus exclusively on getting the job done without distractions is a breath of fresh air.

Project managers are in for a shock

The transition to *agile* should be a natural process, more of a homecoming than a revolution. The only shock in store is for anyone who is a command-and-control style project manager. There's no need for a dictator in a collaborative environment and no place for that approach within an *agile* set-up. One of the most common mistakes made in a fledgling *agile* environment is automatically putting one of the old school project managers (PMs) in charge of the first project.

Of course many PMs successfully navigate the conversion but they're usually closet *agilists* anyway. It's not a new idea for managers to concentrate on getting the best out of the team rather than shouting out orders. Many believe they're only as good as the people around them and see themselves primarily as *enablers* and *facilitators*; furthermore they're no strangers to delegation. That's one of the reasons why there's a strong *it's-just-common-sense* camp concerning *agile* because, yes, it's just common sense for some.

But adopting *agile* is a situation where one bad apple can spoil the whole barrel. There's nothing worse than someone bringing bad habits into a fresh *agile* environment. Project managers never admit to being control freaks or believing in a my-way-or-the-highway approach but that's the way it is most of the time. A very different mind-set is required and it's very hard to change the habits of a lifetime. So be wary of putting a wily old fox in charge of the hen house.

Don't go agile if...

✔ Barking orders and telling people what to do is a huge pleasure

✔ Taking all the credit for the success of others is a way of life

✔ Looking for a scapegoat is the first move when anything hits the fan

✔ Colleagues who enjoy work are treated with suspicion

✔ You think change and flexibility is for wimps.

Not a panacea

Always remember that despite all the good stuff, *agile* isn't a cure-all solution and plenty can go wrong. In this respect, *agile* isn't so different. Ultimately, it provides an approach that will be used and *possibly abused*. This is a big problem to deal with and counter, especially when *agile* is *unintentionally* misrepresented. It's not unheard of for inexperienced practitioners to declare allegiance to the cause without sufficient experience. Ensuring people stay within the spirit of *agile* but leaving them up to their own devices is a pretty big ask.

Not everyone has the right mind-set for using *agile*. For the most part, individuals adapt quickly but there are always those who either never get it or basically don't buy in to it. Sceptics often do an about turn when they see *agile* in action so don't overreact to initial concerns – but they can sometimes prove terminal. As a general rule unbelievers can seriously undermine a team, especially in the early days so don't persevere endlessly. Occasionally things won't work out but don't see it as a flaw with *agile*, or the person concerned.

Yet another way in which *agile* isn't different to other delivery mechanisms is that projects aren't all a perfect match – more

brilliant tip

One of the common side-effects of going *agile* is that pre-existing problems are exposed and the truth comes out, warts and all. Often it also becomes clear that there are some who aren't helping matters by underperforming or just being picky, gossipy, out of touch – you name it.

Agile *is only the whistle-blower, so don't let it take the blame for creating problems in the first place. Be wary of anybody who gets outed as incompetent, especially if they're in the senior management team!*

than most fit the bill but some don't. There's no such thing as one-size-fits-all where project are concerned. Rather than work through a list of reasons to exclude projects, look for the characteristics that are best matched to *agile* including:

- aggressive deadlines;
- a high degree of complexity;
- rampant uncertainty;
- plenty of unknowns;
- unique rather than a repeat order;
- new requests for new features.

At a macro level, there are even organisations that struggle to embrace *agile*. There are set-ups where a rigid and fixed mind-set is engrained into the culture and the huge differences in approach become a terminal blocker. Fortunately that is remarkably rare and a more common situation arises when key individuals don't like what's on offer. Of course, not everyone is going to get the *agile* bug and if the Top Banana is not for turning it will be an uphill struggle.

Classic agile mismatches

✔ **Unsuitable organisation:** don't expect the Navy to go for it.

✔ **Incorrect project:** building an aircraft carrier isn't a match.

✔ **Wrong character mix:** dictators and hermits won't adapt.

The final word

Can you think of a business, company or service that no longer exists or doesn't have the market share it used to have? The recent economic downturn has given us lots of examples: HMV, Blockbuster, Woolworths, Myspace, Nokia and Blackberry, along with many others. Why did seemingly rock-solid businesses fail or dramatically fall from grace? What takes them from being global super-brands to past their sell by date overnight?

There are also those that don't collapse outright but lose their way. Tesco isn't the only darling of the stock market to issue a series of profit warnings or to see someone steal its thunder. Lost opportunities are just as bad as outright disasters and there are many reoccurring reasons for either happening. Maybe the financial downturn hit sales or perhaps products simply fell out of favour. Or perhaps someone else found a way to execute *faster, cheaper, better*. There's often a common thread when it all goes pear shaped: a reluctance or inability to change.

Agile helps find a way forward quickly *and* at the right price. It doesn't come with a magic wand but if you're standing at the crossroads like Tesco, then *every little helps*. At its very core, *agile* is just an umbrella term for the tools and techniques that allow you to practise *agility* – the ability to be flexible and respond to change. But always bear in mind that although *agile* is different, it isn't *perfect*. There will be many situations where things don't quite work out as planned. Expect to win some and lose some. Aim to win the war, not every battle.

brilliant recap

- Change is a fact of life: don't be a dinosaur.
- Comprehensive, complex processes only keep things on track if you're heading to a *fixed* destination.
- There's no such thing as a cure-all and *agile* isn't for everyone... especially some project managers.
- *Agility* is the ability to be flexible and respond to change.
- Maybe *agile* isn't new but it's *very* different!

CHAPTER 3

Getting ready: preparing to be *agile*

Introduction

Many traditional project management methodologies are based on dotting all the i's and crossing all the t's before setting off. Project requirements are drafted and redrafted, reviewed, revised, revamped and examined from every possible angle before any *real* work is done – whereas there's a view in some circles that *agile* is all about making it up as you go along, starting off with a vague idea and then winging it.

Nothing could be further from the truth. Yes it's true that the first goal is to get feedback quickly on a basic release. Yes, it's also true that subsequent deliveries build on that foundation. And yes it's very true that there's plenty of flexibility along the way to make adjustments or even completely change track if necessary. However, this is done in a considered way based on a vision of the final destination and always for good *business reasons*.

It's very easy to confuse flexibility with a scattergun approach but *agile* is a far more considered approach to project delivery than traditional methods, not the other way around. Less effort is put in before setting off and it's more wisely invested. There's a world of difference in what gets done first and instead of trying to pin everything down, *agile* puts in place a framework that delivers early and builds steadily from there.

Agile ensures the end goal is defined up front and an enabling infrastructure is put in place for getting there but worries little about the fine detail of the journey before setting off.

Luck is where opportunity meets preparation.

Denzel Washington

Defining the vision

Without a vision, the people will perish. Moses said that about 4,000 years ago and from the looks of it most project managers still don't know what he was getting at. If we don't know where we're going, we won't get there and this is especially true with projects. That's because people will make all sorts of assumptions about what it is we're trying to do, interpret things differently and drive towards different results. Having a clear vision is essential.

Unfortunately many visions go the way of bad *mission statements* and seem to say much but once put under the microscope reveal very little:

● We want to offer unparalleled quality.

● We aim to put our customers first and deliver value.

● We will be the best at what we do and loved by everyone everywhere.

Nice sentiments but ultimately useless. You can't deliver against them. You can't use them to know when you've done the business.

Defining a project vision

✔ What is the name of the project or product you are making?

✔ Who is it for?

✔ When will it be done by?

✔ What will it do?

✔ What will it not do?

✔ What benefit does your business get for doing it?

✔ What benefit does your customer get by using it?

Write the vision in a way that your Mum or Dad can understand what you're planning to do.

A vision should be a tool that you can use. You can use it to communicate intent. You can use it to explain what you are doing and what you are *not* doing. You can use it to prioritise against. A vision for a project should be less of a strategic mission statement for the business and more of a tactical, practical device to help you stay focused. A vision must be open to change and get updated *when* it goes stale, which it surely will.

As an example of how to use a vision, let's imagine that we're an existing company that wants to start selling organic vegetable boxes to our restaurateur customers. A vision can help us define exactly what that means:

> By the end of September, Project VegBox will develop a new iOS app that lets our customers order from a premium range of 10 veg box products for their restaurants, to be delivered with their regular orders. By offering this, our business gets to grow the veg department by creating a new product line and our customers have an easy and convenient way to get organic veg at wholesale prices.

The vision explains what we are planning to do. It's quite specific about the target group, platform, and product – plus when the project will be done by. Most importantly, it talks about the value delivered to both the business and the end customer.

brilliant example

A family day out doesn't need to be planned with military precision. It's more than enough to agree on the basics: the destination, what to take and how to get there. There's no need to agree a minute-by-minute itinerary before setting off and limited value in considering every possible

▶

what-if scenario. The main thing to get right is whether you're going to a theme park, heading for a relaxing day on the beach or a day shopping.

If the end destination is agreed, the rest is just about the logistics of getting there.

Driven by business value

Too many projects start off with a half-baked notion. Someone in a position of influence or with a budget to burn comes up with a brainwave and before anybody knows it there is an unstoppable juggernaut heading for who knows where. Of course, projects are never openly acknowledged as whims, but don't assume the foundations are solid just on the back of a persuasive senior manager or the enthusiasm of the company clever clogs. Carry out due diligence and never assume that a sensible investment decision has been made.

Agile is totally focused on delivering *business value*. From the start of any project and all along the way, the business team will know exactly what they're getting for their money.

 **brilliant** definition

People say they want to *deliver value* so often that it can become almost meaningless. What does *value* mean? Think in terms of *benefit*. What *benefit* does this bring to the customer or the business? The most successful projects provide business value to both.

Agile doesn't dictate the definition of *business value* and to a large degree beauty is in the eye of the beholder; it provides a framework for ensuring the business think through what it wants for its hard-earned cash without in any way dictating to it what constitutes a wise investment. *Agile* facilitates and enables sensible decisions and nothing more. It takes the horse to water but doesn't force it to drink.

Every delivery, every feature, every nuance must be described in business-speak. Gone are the days of a person or persons unknown defining a list of requirements in technobabble or a foreign language the business doesn't fully understand before lighting the blue touch paper and retiring to a safe place. Long gone are the days of the business putting its blind faith in people they hardly know. With *agile* the business describes what it wants and then works within the project team to ensure the vision is delivered exactly as requested.

Not only that, the business will define exactly what's needed as a *minimum* to get going and every additional chunk needed from there on in. The first delivery may not have many bells and whistles but will be usable, deliver value and it will arrive sooner rather than later. It will be crystal clear that for an investment of X then Y gets delivered initially and ditto for every subsequent delivery down the line.

brilliant tip

If you don't know what it is you're building (the vision), what benefit it will bring (value proposition) or who it's for (end user proposition), then you can have the best experts in the world and yet never deliver anything worthwhile.

Building the project team

Many people stress themselves silly by building a high-quality project team, finding the best people they can to get the job done – people with proven experience, experts in their fields – and then fail to give them adequate business and leadership.

Talk about putting the cart before the horse! The importance of getting the right level of business involvement – one empowered individual who understands the business vision – is not just practical and pragmatic, but pure common sense.

With *agile* this person is known most commonly as the *Product Owner* but there are variations on the theme. *Product Management* is worthy of a *Brilliant* book in its own right but for the sake of getting started let's keep it simple. A Product Owner represents the needs of the business and the users. Product Owners live, breathe and dream about the product and what it will be. They know *what* they want even if they don't know *how* it will be done. They are leaders, able to make decisions quickly and stand by them even in the face of opposition.

The *agile* team is a diverse, cross-functional group of individuals that has the ability and authority to deliver the vision on behalf of the business. Put simply, between them they have everything they need to get the job done properly. The Product Owner leads the way in terms of the business vision but it's very much a team effort. The team consists of people who have an *agile* mind-set, who are not afraid of change and don't need to use process and bureaucracy as a crutch to get by. Confident decision makers with a self-starter, can-do attitude are the best for this.

Collectively the team must buy into the vision and co-own all aspects of the project delivery. If that isn't the case, there'll be big trouble ahead.

Creating a backlog

Once there is a practical vision in place and the business value is established, the next step is for the project team to pin down in more detail what's required. At the heart of any project is this type of requirements list and with *agile* this is known as

Ways to get off on the wrong foot

✔ Proclaim *agile* as the only answer - either join the gang or hit the highway.

✔ Announce that it's all obvious - any idiot can pick it up, so no training is required.

✔ Declare *agile* is infallible - failures will be solely down to personal inadequacies.

✔ Dictate unreasonable targets and deadlines - explain that nothing is impossible in this brave new *agile* world.

the *product backlog*. It replaces the traditional, detailed, requirements-specification type approach and is in the form of a shopping list of ideas that's meaningful to the business. Items on the backlog are always user-centric even if they have a technical slant. The litmus test is that they make sense to pretty much anyone.

A sensible place to start is for the project team to dig into the vision statement as a group – to make sure everyone understands it, its scope and what it's helping us to conceptualise. Making sure all parties are on the same page from the start is much easier than trying to fix a broken project two-thirds of the way through the process. The diversity of the team is important, as they need to think about the project from all different angles. If necessary, specialists can be drafted in to help out.

Define primary functionality

The aim is to produce a summary list of what's needed to deliver the project vision. There are several ways to do this and our favourite approach is to think about each step of the customer journey to produce a *workflow*.

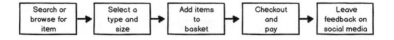

Produce feature groups

Once the workflow is mapped out, gather together ideas about what's actually *done* within each step in the journey. Added together these items deliver the functionality of the step and are often referred to as *feature groups*. Some of the items will be absolutely essential and some nice-to-haves. To begin with get all the thoughts down.

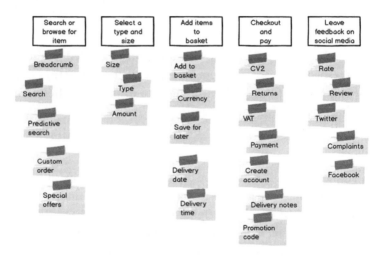

Prioritising the features

Using the value statement in the project vision and common business sense prioritise the ideas, in descending order with the most valuable item at the top of each list.

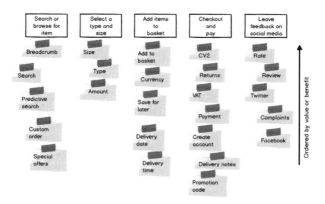

Identify the first delivery

Once that's done think about whether each step in the customer journey is vital from Day 1 and what's the most valuable chunk of ideas within those steps. This selection process can be challenging and at the end of the day a matter of opinion, but the business, or whoever represents the needs of the business, is the best judge of all this. The end result is the minimum the project must achieve to deliver a useable outcome. This is usually referred to as the *minimum viable product (MVP)* or the *minimum viable release (MVR)*.

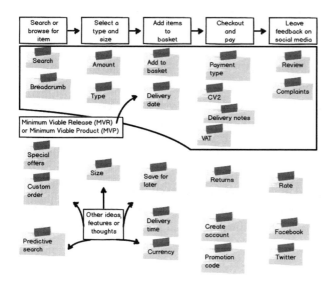

One of the biggest hooks for *agile* working is to get fast, meaningful feedback from the end customers and they need something tangible to provide an opinion about. It's not possible to get meaningful feedback on any new under-the-bonnet techie infrastructure, for example, but it is possible to get feedback on a new VegBox order form. This would naturally be part of the MVP.

We need to be aware that the more there is in an MVP, the longer it will take to get feedback, whereas if we put too little in it, there will not be enough information to get feedback on. You have to strike the balance between return and risk – there's no golden rule. Try to find the point where you get good feedback on something useful, something that will help you make informed decisions. It can pay dividends to carry out market analysis beforehand.

Beware of *loaded* terms too. For some the word *release* means a publicly available product. For others it means something to see and test out on a closed audience. Remember, it's possible to release in little bits to a closed group and then, once this has built up, do a proper public release. Don't make assumptions that everyone means the same thing! No one approach is right, so pick the one that works best for you.

Adding features

Once the MVP or MVR or whatever you want to call the first delivery is out there, the *real* fun begins. Additional functionality or even specific features can be delivered in bite-sized chunks or packaged up into bigger releases. This is called *incremental delivery*.

Businesses love incremental delivery. No more waiting for years and years for one huge delivery containing every imaginable bell and whistle. The *agile* delivery preference is for little and often. There is a balancing act here once again but the business decides *what* and *when*. The smallest possible delivery is one solitary feature that can be validated through practical use.

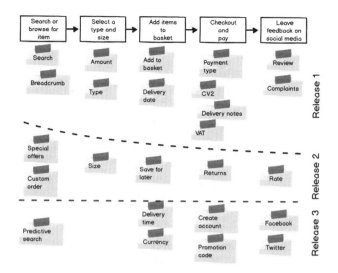

Getting more information

So far the items in the first release, our MVP, are very lightweight and we'll need to get more detail on them. The reason they're high level at this point is because we're trying to formulate ideas and it's wasteful to elaborate requirements that may not go on to be used. That was more than enough to define the big picture and agree the MVP but not enough to get on with the work itself.

The next step is to get more information on everything earmarked for the first release. The classic tool for capturing further details is the *user story*.

Tell me a story

User stories are short, simple description of a feature told from the perspective of the person who desires the new capability, usually a user or customer of the system. They typically follow a simple format:

As a <type of user>, I want <some goal> so that <reason>.

Title	Assign a clear and concise title. This is a great way to summarise, index and search for stories.
As a <type of user>	We need to know who the end user will be. Who this feature is for.
I want <some goal>	What is the functionality the end user wants? Describe the 'what' not the 'how'.
So that <reason>	What is the reason for needing this feature (with some kind of business or customer benefit here)?

A user story is a very high-level definition, containing just enough information so that the team can produce a reasonable estimate of the effort to do the actual work. User stories are often written on index cards or sticky notes, stored and arranged on walls or wherever there's a space to facilitate planning and further discussion. They shift the focus from writing reams about features to discussing them.

A user story isn't a requirement. It is defined as *a reminder to have a conversation* and these discussions are often more important than whatever's written. It is these dialogues that

DELIVERY DATE
AS A NON-REGULAR CUSTOMER
I WANT A GUARANTEED DELIVERY
DATE WHEN I PLACE MY ORDER
SO THAT I KNOW WHEN TO
EXPECT MY ORDER, SO THAT IT
DOESN'T ROT ON THE DOORSTEP

spark the most important thinking points about the *requirement*. Remember, anything written today that won't get started on for a while can go stale. However, if we just gather enough detail to have a *meaningful* conversation, the reminder stays fresh and time isn't wasted penning copious detail. Win–win.

Pin down acceptance criteria

How do we know when we are done? It's a key question and the first one that should be asked when starting a conversation prompted by a user story. In order to work efficiently, it's important to know when to stop. What are the boundaries of the work? How much do we do for it to be accepted? How will we avoid over-egging or gold plating the requirements? For a user story to be truly done it needs *acceptance criteria* – the prerequisites that have to be met for a story to be assessed as complete.

Acceptance criteria can take many forms, from simple *conditions of satisfaction* all the way through to rigorous and very exact checks. For the purposes of getting *agile*, simple binary statements written in plain language are the best place to start. Let's take the *delivery date user story* a little further by writing some simple acceptance tests for it:

- The delivery date will always be the next working day.
- The delivery date will be on a Monday if the order is placed on a Saturday.
- The delivery date cut-off time for orders will be 3pm.
- There will be email confirmation of the delivery date.
- All product lines have the same delivery date rules.
- We can never specify a time of delivery, only the day.
- The user can leave a note for the delivery driver.
- The anticipated delivery day will be shown on the screen when ordering.

Acceptance criteria written collaboratively by the team is the most likely way to cover all the angles. Led by the *Product Owner* or business representative, the team can talk through the stories, remove ambiguity and pin down the end game. These sessions are the best way to bring about team alignment and they don't need to be long, or laborious. They can be done *just in time* to start work; the aim is to start with the end in mind!

As a by-product, acceptance criteria provide a useful measurement to report progress against. Frequently, business confidence is undermined though being vague: '*I think we're nearly done*' or '*I feel we're on track*'. So these checks are an aid to being more precise by providing specific and measurable milestones: *we're halfway through the acceptance criteria*. This type of gauge will be easily achievable if the checks are properly formatted and alarm bells should be ringing if not.

Splitting stories

Sometimes, too much of a *good conversation* generates an over-abundance of material. Don't worry, this is a good thing – don't stop the dialogue, capture it all. Some ideas may be not appropriate for the story you're working through or may be too advanced for it. Not to worry, as once captured they can be filtered. Some of it can be added to other more appropriate stories.

Others may call for a new story to be written and this is known as *splitting a story*. A common example is where the Product Owner sees some of the acceptance criteria as unnecessary for the time being and wants to create a new story for the extended features – to be reminded to talk about them in the future. Once the new story is written, it can just be prioritised into the backlog along with everything else.

Keeping user stories to a manageable size is important. The more complex a story is, the more risk of something going horribly wrong. Huge reams of acceptance criteria are an indicator that a story has gone that way and *must* be split. There are times when this needs to happen multiple times and it's a legitimate way of breaking work down into reasonable-sized work packages.

Yes, size matters

Now we have a vision, a backlog, an MVP and some well-written user stories complete with acceptance criteria. Great stuff. The next step to ask then is: *how much work is all that?* Traditionally project managers or specialist estimators carry out this task and then throw their predictions over the fence. But on an *agile* project the team, the people actually doing the work, produce the estimates. Apart from the huge benefit of more reliable projections, there's the advantage of getting team buy-in.

Of course the size of each user story is required to predict when the MVP will initially be delivered and when the subsequent other features. But this is also a way of being forewarned of potential problems with individual pieces of work – head scratching, big intakes of breath and shaking heads are sure-fire signs of trouble ahead.

There are several estimating techniques well suited to *agile* projects and the following are worth considering:

- **T-shirt sizing.** Assign S, M, L, XL and XXL tags to everything and gauge roughly how much work each size involves. Easy to use and a good starter-for-ten but can lack precision.

- **Story pointing.** Use a Fibonacci scale for all the pieces of work in hand – for example from 1 to 100 points – where 1 is easy-peasy and 100 a raised eyebrow moment. Takes some getting used to but there are many devoted fans.

- **Affinity prioritisation**. Sequence all of the stories in order of relative size – shuffling stories into smallest to largest order – and assign 1 to the smallest and the relative size to the next biggest and so on. Useful for getting to grips with the MVP.

The easy road to ropey estimates

✔ Start with an incomplete backlog.

✔ Vague *user stories* are a must.

✔ Big, complex, multifunctional stories add spice.

✔ Be optimistic and hope for the best.

✔ If in doubt just guess.

✔ Don't worry... estimates are usually wildly wrong anyway.

Less is more

Outside of the *agile* world there's normally a cat and mouse game played at the start of a project. The business team know instinctively they have to ask for everything under the sun because there's only one shot at getting *most* of what they need. They also know that when things start to go pear shaped – as they regularly do in some form or other – the deliverables are going to be pared back. So it's better to ask for the kitchen sink to improve the negotiating position.

Project teams know this goes on of course and are happy to have wiggle room built in for when the times get tough. The problem is that when the squeeze hits, many of the bells and whistles have already been delivered and it's too late to recapture that poorly invested effort. When the budget dries up or time runs out, the remaining work includes many non-negotiable essentials: for example, within a house renovation project, having a very high-spec kitchen with all the latest lighting and gizmos when the bathroom is still a bare shell.

Of course it's common sense to start by delivering a barebones solution and build from there but there needs to be an understanding that the plug isn't pulled after initial delivery. There needs to be faith that there will be incremental deliveries from there on, building and honing the final product. Although much depends on trust, the whole ethos of an *agile* project is based on this premise, so nothing can go wrong unless the whole set-up is a total sham – which even *agile* can't insure against.

The *MVP* is the absolute minimum required just to get going. Every feature and nuance is non-negotiable without any nice-to-haves. The litmus test for anything on the first to-do list is that the whole MVP would be unusable without its inclusion. In practice, it doesn't matter too much if a couple of minor bits 'n pieces sneak in as long as the traditional gold plating doesn't happen. The objective is to end up with a lean, mean set of requirements that can be delivered quickly.

Once business teams and customers go through the loop, they immediately get how much better this works for them. The reduced time-to-market is a big winner and the key to competitive advantage. Plus, in practice it's usually very hard to predict the optimum final outcome and much easier to add to a working product. It is interesting to look back on any nice-to-haves after the first delivery is in place as normally other more important features come into contention. There's nothing stopping the team from having a long list of features waiting for the production line.

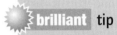 **tip**

Finance teams aren't usually leading the charge to go _agile_ but they quickly get on board when the benefits are explained properly. A reduced time-to-market, incremental delivery and an early return on investment is music to their ears. The end to ever-spiralling budgets alone is enough to win them over. Very powerful allies.

Risk and expectation management

Done properly, there's no risk of _typical_ problems occurring on an _agile_ project because risk management and mitigation is built into the framework – greater all-round visibility with a diverse team of specialists on hand helps enormously. The main risk with _agile_ is going off-piste in some way or another:

- **Don't deviate from tried and tested practices.** Many people try to change too much, too frequently. Stick with the guidelines and make adjustments one at a time. If your changes don't work, drop them!
- **Communicate, communicate and communicate.** Bad communication is the root of all evil. Leaving information out is as misleading as giving bad information. Use the _backlogs_ as the focus for regularly having the right conversations at the right time.

- **Avoid large work items.** The larger requirements are, the harder they are to understand. Break down any big items into smaller, more manageable chunks.

- **Keep talking.** The best way to manage *agile* risk is by continually having meaningful conversations with those people around you. Let them all talk!

---

brilliant tip

One of the biggest risks of failure is in only paying lip service to the *agile* framework and becoming an ordinary project in disguise.

Be wary of sheep in wolf's clothing.

Managing the backlog

It's hard to over-emphasise how important the backlog is. It is the cornerstone of your project. However, a good backlog can go bad very quickly if it's left unattended. The backlog *has* to be living, breathing and attention-seeking. Used well they're brilliant at helping to demystify what is coming up, helping communication with others, reducing risk and managing expectations. If they are neglected, they become a time-consuming distraction that sends people off course fast. Keep the *backlog* up to date!

At the start of a project, a backlog is usually full of functional requirements and features written as user stories. As the project moves on it will become filled with other items and a user story is just one form of *product backlog item*. Backlogs need to make all work visible and that includes faults, non-functional requirements, improvements, enhancements, new feature requests – everything. Get them all written down and blend them in with everything else, ordering them by *business value* just as always.

The backlog belongs to the Product Owner, who remains accountable for it at all times. As such they should be constantly *refining* it by using it as the main focal point for discussions with all interested parties. Keeping the backlog up to date is hard work, but the benefit pays off through the visibility it provides and the conversations it initiates. Transparency builds trust on projects, and by far the best way to achieve this is to make your continually refined backlog visible to all.

The best way to make sure that your backlog is up to date is to get the team and Product Owner to look at it every day. This can be part of a daily routine or part of any exercise where the team talk about what they're doing. Sometimes, the Product Owner spends a lot of time refining the backlog, sometimes just minutes. The important thing is that it's being used and referred to regularly.

 **brilliant** tip

A static backlog is a sure-fire sign of trouble. Keep an eye out for prolonged inactivity.

Creating the right environment

Success on an *agile* project is more about the individuals and the interactions between them working than anything else. It's hard to get people working together efficiently and their environment is crucial in promoting effective communications. The most successful *agile* teams are product focused, sit together and have easy access to their Product Owner. Plus they're in sight of both the team task board and most crucially the *product backlog*. A team that sits together has fewer obstacles in the way of communicating, interacting or even just building rapport by chatting about the weekend.

Let's be realistic though. It's easy to say we should all sit together, laugh, work, be funny and good looking – but in reality people make long commutes, companies have offices in different cities and partnerships with off-site teams too. Whatever the circumstances, visibility, transparency, communication and interactions collaboration is key and quite often we need help to achieve this. Video conferencing, electronic task boards on giant touch-screen TVs, conference calling are never brilliant but *always* better than nothing. If, and it's a big if, there's a well-maintained and refined practical backlog, these tools can work.

There's no excuse for the team being uncertain about their objectives, what's coming up next and the part they have to play in it *whatever the physical circumstances.* If a team isn't communicating, it means something is seriously wrong and the bitter truth is teams usually perform badly as a consequence of a bad environment. We agree there's undisputed value in good communications and where there's a will there's a way.

 If you don't know where you're going, you'll end up someplace else.

Yogi Berra

The final word

Starting a project with a muddled vision plays right into the hands of the anti-*agile* brigade because, if so, it really will be a case of making it up as you go along. Defining a target of substance sets the scene for everything that follows. Even the best teams in the world can't deliver successfully if they're blindfolded from the beginning. Starting with the end in mind is harder than it sounds but it's non-negotiable.

Once that foundation stone is in place it's not all plain sailing through. Building a rock-steady *backlog* is the next key target, but luckily it's not an onerous task creating an exhaustive, detailed list of requirements. No need to disappear for a lengthy period of time and produce reams of documentation supporting a gold-plated monolith. Knocking the backlog into shape is a relatively quick, shared experience and – can you believe it – great fun.

Finally, on an _agile_ project the first delivery milestone isn't a life sentence. The initial target will be set at the bare minimum to get the business going and nothing more. This will happen quickly with the promise that from then on the deliveries will come fast and furious. No more promises of _mañana_ for things to begin kicking into gear. Watch the business purring and getting ready to revel in a brave new _agile_ world.

brilliant recap

- Start with a specific and _meaningful_ vision; no waffle or vague targets.

- Business value is everything, so develop a shared understanding of what it really means.

- _Love thy backlog._ Develop a top quality backlog with rock-solid stories that can be understood by everyone.

- Pin down that MVP! Everything rests on getting it right and out there quickly.

- Always works out the _acceptance criteria_ up front; start with the end in mind.

CHAPTER 4

Using Kanban

Introduction

There's a whole host of reasons for wanting to adopt an *agile* approach. Perhaps projects are regularly stumbling along or even consistently failing to deliver the goods. Or maybe the excellent word-of-mouth about *agile* is an incentive. The road leading to an *agile* world will vary but once the desire is there, the big questions are where to start and how complex the initial step is going to be.

There are several options for making the first leap. There's nothing to stop a big bang approach and there are many examples of successful overnight revolutions. But there are many situations where a softly-softly approach is preferred and there's nothing wrong with starting by dipping a toe in the water. There are many ways to do this in an *agile* context and one excellent option is to introduce Kanban.

Kanban – literally translated from Japanese means a signboard or billboard – started life as a scheduling system in the motor industry and is now one of the fastest growth areas in the *agile* market. It's easy to grasp, simple to implement and costs pretty much nothing. A big advantage to Kanban is that it can be used by individuals or teams to manage their workload or on full-scale projects.

Don't be fooled into thinking Kanban isn't the real McCoy and is merely a stepping-stone to Scrum. Yes, it can be part of the *agile* journey rather than the final destination but Kanban is an excellent framework in its own right. Kanban isn't the coward's way out or a soft option. It's a brilliant introduction to working in an *agile* way and there's more to it than meets the eye.

 Life is a gamble. If you want something badly, you'd have to trust your heart and your instincts and then take a leap of faith.

Alyssa Urbano

Kanban fundamentals

Kanban started life as a scheduling system for assembly lines in the automobile industry. Kanban was developed as a framework to maintain a high level of production at Toyota by managing the workflow with fine-tuning and self-improvement built in. Over time Kanban has morphed into a more general pipeline process and is used in a variety of business sectors.

Kanban hasn't strayed from the original philosophy; it has merely been enhanced and adapted over the years into a highly credible *agile* process. The original simplicity of the underpinning concepts remains the big attraction and at the heart of Kanban is the concept that all work starts life as *to-do* and ends up as *done*. It's all about building an effective way of getting from A to Z.

This is about evolution, not revolution. Kanban encourages teams to begin with the current status quo and build from there by consulting the people directly involved in the process. Change is therefore consensual, thus increasing the likelihood of Kanban being adopted enthusiastically. There are three guiding principles that sum it all up:

1 Start with what you do now.
2 Agree to pursue incremental, evolutionary change.
3 Respect the current process, roles, responsibilities and titles.

brilliant tip

Be wary if the call to move to Kanban is from a team already using one of the other *agile* frameworks.

It can be a sign of pure genius because Kanban is very much underrated in some circles and there's a great deal of subtlety embedded in the seemingly simplistic processes. But there are some who've heard that there's no planning or estimating in Kanban and found that so boring with Scrum or whatever they're currently using; so jumping ship is very appealing.

Moving on for the wrong reasons usually ends in tears in any aspect of life. Including moving to Kanban.

Stripped down to basics, there are five key steps for implementing Kanban: starting with producing a visual representation of the end-to-end flow of work, then placing constraints on the amount of work in play at any one moment in time plus finally steps to measure and improve the efficiency of the flow.

1 **Visualise workflow.** Kick off with a visual representation of the flow of work going from to-do to done status. Many prefer to add only one other step in between: in progress. Others prefer to break the workflow down into a series of procedural stages such as: plan, design, draft, build, test, deploy, with to-do and done as bookends.

2 **Limit work-in-progress.** Trying to do too many things at the same time is a proven recipe for disaster; it applies equally at an individual level and to teams. Kanban limits the number of items allowed to be on the go at any one time – known as the work-in-progress (WiP) – to ensure optimum efficiency. Common sense is enough to get started and then experience will help fine tune to pin down the optimal WiP limit.

3 **Manage the flow of work.** The aim is to achieve a fast, smooth movement from to-do to done. If so it means the process is operating at optimum efficiency thus creating maximum business value in the shortest time possible. An important add-on is for it to be repeatable and consistent.

4 **Make the process explicit.** An unambiguous statement of how work gets done is essential for any objective review. With a common understanding it's easier to discuss issues impartially and reach a consensus on improvements. There must be a natural checkpoint at the end of each step with clear rules for moving on to the next one.

5 **Improve collaboratively.** Once the spotlight is on the workflow, ideas start to develop about how it can be improved. The WiP limit plays a key role in sparking discussions by forcing the team to focus on blockers to work in play when the limit is reached. An initial cap of no more than two tasks per person soon highlights problems that impede the flow; then the team simply faces up to those issues and resolves them.

Kanban's great for:

- Getting off to a low-risk, zero-cost, *agile,* fast start.
- Pinning down existing workflows and spotting glaring errors.
- Controlling multiple pieces of unconnected work.
- Keeping the numbers of jobs in play down to an acceptable level.
- Getting the team into an *agile* way of thinking.

All aboard

At the heart of the Kanban method is a deceptively clever tool: the Kanban board. Calling these boards a visual to-do list is an over-simplification but a decent starting point. The board is a graphic representation of the work to be done and the end-to-end flow from start to finish. The simplest and some argue the most pure Kanban board consists of just three columns: things *to do*, tasks *in progress* and finally work *done*. This simple format is universal and matches any project or corporate workflow.

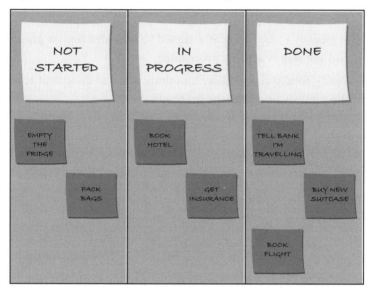

Figure 4.1 The Kanban board

After a while it's natural to be more thoughtful about the typical workflow of tasks and consider whether there are other steps en route to *job done* status. A popular variation on the theme is to separate out *ideas* that are being considered but are not yet definite runners. It's also worth breaking down the work-in-progress especially if more than one person along the way handles tasks. There must be a noticeable and measurable change in the status of work between each step in the process.

Keep it simple to start with and try out the four previously suggested stages: *ideas, to do, doing* and *done*. The demarcation between each status is clear and in turn generates the triggers for moving cards on:

1 *Ideas* – the *maybe or maybe not* stage when there's a question mark of any sort outstanding.

2 *To do* or *in progress* – when an idea is thought through and the only questions are who is going to do the work and when will it start.

3 *In progress* – once work is assigned to an individual or group and the task is actively proceeding.

4 *Done* – totally complete with nothing more to do except reap the rewards or accept the gratitude.

▶ brilliant example

The Sunday Times Fast Track 100 is a list published annually each December in the UK. It ranks Britain's fastest growing privately held companies by sales growth over the last three years.

When one of these companies came up for sale, the interest was intense. Everyone agreed the company was a diamond and a bidding war ensued. As part of the standard corporate due diligence each investor went on a tour of the offices and production facilities led by one of the management team. The tours weren't scripted but each senior manager cruised by the Kanban board for one of the strategic internal projects and spent a few minutes explaining how it worked.

It's not only profit and loss columns that illustrate the potential of a forward thinking company.

The definition of done

One of the biggest challenges for any style of project management is pinning down the *job done* status work. It is essential to pin down the final exit criteria – also known as the *definition of done* – for each task up front to avoid disputes down the line. Be precise about the criteria for accepting the delivery and settling the bill. There are often genuine misunderstandings about what's in and what's not and *agile* pays particular attention to this universal phenomenon.

Engaging the customer or business is the only way to do this properly; yet another common sense idea at the heart of *agile* philosophy. For example, this is easy when dealing with retailers or local trades people – probably as a result of previous experience. When you order a new dishwasher from an electrical store, does the quote include delivery and installation? Are you expected to turn up with a van or does the deal include everything, including a quick demo of the basic functions? When the local plumber comes in with an excellent deal for the bathroom of your dreams, is the deal inclusive of the finishing touches like tiling and grouting?

Pinning down the *definition of done* is a collaborative process and there's usually an element of trial and error involved. Don't wing it; set adequate time aside to come up with the final exit criteria but don't agonise too much either. Running a few tasks through the process will iron out any small kinks.

brilliant tip

Never move a task in to *done* status prematurely *for any reason*. Work that is nearly there or – even worse 99% complete – isn't *done* yet. Hold fire even when the pressure is on to show progress.

More than just a board

Once the starting format of the Kanban board is agreed, the first and almost pivotal decision to be made is whether to go for a physical board or an electronic one. Both have their pros and cons and there may be working practices that guide the final decision. A virtual board can't be beaten for accessibility and ease of sharing, as you're never more than a smart phone or iPad away. But in our opinion the most important thing is for the board to be highly visible, and nothing can beat a physical board for that.

A high-profile, physical board has an almost magical quality, like a fireplace in a huge front room, and draws people in. To start with it's more about curiosity, yet after a short while it becomes a centrepiece and focus for team activities. Work is planned, prioritised and progressed around the board. A physical board is also guaranteed to generate huge interest in unlikely places. Senior management *love* the visibility of a board, so expect a visit from the CEO or Finance Director within a week. For once they'll see what's really going on in the organisation without quizzing middle management or ploughing through turgid weekly reports.

An old-fashioned corkboard, note cards, pens and pins are enough to begin with. Or a very popular variation on the theme is a whiteboard and sticky notes. Perhaps try to make better use of that existing noticeboard with an 18-month-old, indecipherable diagram and a do-not-remove warning. At a push a Kanban board only needs to accommodate three or four columns to start with but always try to begin with enough physical capacity to allow for expansion.

Put the board in a central location and avoid rarely visited outposts at all costs. Be prepared to de-clutter to get a prime spot if necessary. The board will soon become a hive of activity so ensure there's plenty of standing room around it. Without doubt, a physical board will soon be considered a breath of fresh air.

Be bold. Make a public statement. We're going *agile*.

 **example**

How to build the perfect Kanban board:

- Buy 2 rolls of 3 × 1 metre brightly coloured gripper felt, a 50 pack of multi-coloured 6 × 4 inch cards and 6 dry wipe pens.

- Identify a central, prominent wall that the whole project team can see at all times with 2 or 3 metres of usable wall space and enough room for several people to stand in front of it.

- Load the 2 strips of gripper felt lengthways across the wall, 1 directly above the other.

- Divide the resulting 6 × 2 metre felt-fest vertically into 4 columns with half-inch wide ribbon in a contrasting colour.

- Put a card at the top of each column titled: *Ideas, To do, In progress, Done.*

- Leave plenty of space to expand and adjust the number of columns to match steps in the workflow; the board will change and evolve.

- Write up the task cards on the 6 × 4 inch cards and load them into either the *Ideas* column or the *To do* column.

- Shuffle around the cards in the *To do* column until they're in a sensible sequence based on their priority.

- *You're off!*

Low cost, high-tech alternatives

Despite our absolute preference for an old-fashioned physical board, there are times when an electronic board either makes more sense or is even the only viable option. When individuals are regularly on the move or if the team is split over different locations, there are insurmountable physical issues to deal with and a tech option become more attractive.

But before giving up on having a physical board think carefully, especially when trialling *agile* for the first time. A tech alternative will work well enough from a functional perspective but is far less visible and engaging, so many soft benefits will be lost. Don't go down that route just because members of the team occasionally work from home. Don't throw the baby out with the bathwater.

If an electronic board is the only workable solution, consider driving it from a physical source – start with a wall and duplicate. The overhead of keeping two boards in sync will be offset by the benefits of having a *real* board. But when all else fails there are plenty of electronic options with good coverage across the main devices. Some are completely free and all the rest offer a trial period, so try before you buy.

 **timesaver**

Electronic Scrum and Kanban boards are big business, so there's plenty to choose from. *Trello* is free, has excellent device coverage and is extremely easy to use. *JIRA* is more than a board and *agile* practitioners seem to either love it or hate it – there's an option to buy an add-on that prints *user stories* making it very easy to have a synced-up physical board too, giving the best of both worlds.

Building a backlog of work

At the very heart of the Kanban board are the *to-do* items also known as the *backlog* in various *agile* frameworks. These individual items are all delivery focused and must deliver business value directly or indirectly. For example, setting up a Kanban board is a legitimate item but a meeting to discuss the options is merely part of the main job. The tasks are business delivery focused and not centred on activities. If an item on the backlog does not contribute to business goals, it should be removed.

A Kanban *backlog* is very similar to other *agile* work stacks, certainly in the way tasks are captured as user stories. However, there are subtle, yet important, differences with Kanban:

- **All work is of a similar size**. It's better to have smaller stories of roughly equal size. Splitting large pieces of work down into smaller, similar sized packages has been proven to improve workflow and results in more predictive end-to-end cycle times. Comparing like-for-like can also aid the review process.

- **The backlog is refined more regularly.** The Kanban backlog tends to be exceptionally dynamic especially in a support type environment. Backlogs in other *agile* environments are far from static but they're just a touch less zippy. It's not unusual to review a Kanban backlog on a daily basis.

- **Jobs are pulled not pushed.** A Kanban team adopts a *what's next* policy rather than packaging up work into a connected delivery. The task assigned the highest priority is pulled into play when resource becomes available.

brilliant tip

When it comes to introducing *agile*, it's not always plain sailing and it can be a long walk home. At times even getting the nod for a pilot project using *agile* techniques is an impossible dream. If you're up against considerable anti-*agile* sentiment – usually for all the wrong reasons – don't despair. Start small and begin a crusade with *personal* Kanban by starting up your own board. It will provide instant visibility of all aspects of your work for colleagues and put an end to enquiries for status updates from further up the food chain.

Win over the doubters by showing them Personal Kanban in action.

Shuffle the deck

Once all the ideas are thought through and the *to-do* list or *backlog* shapes up, the next step is to get work into a sensible sequence. Nobody in their right minds wades through their *backlog* in alphabetical order but it's surprising how many fall into a somewhat random approach, such as picking up whatever takes your fancy or responding to peer pressure or even a bit of both. It's surprising how many jobs are selected *just because* rather than for a scientific reason.

A core concept within all *agile* variants is the goal to be driven by business value, and simplistically that's the primary basis for assigning work priority. Work that delivers the most value gets launched before anything providing marginal benefits. Layered on top of this key driver is an assessment of the cost of delivery – if two things deliver the same value, it's common sense to deliver the easiest one first.

Don't get too hung up assigning business value as a comparative assessment is enough. In this context it's all about the relative importance of work, not a detailed analysis. Carry out a similar exercise for the cost of delivery, including all the relevant factors such as timescales, days of effort and hard cash involved. Multiply the two assessments together to get a total score that drives the priority sequence.

---

brilliant example

There are five simple steps for pinning down priorities:

- Rationalise the backlog into standard size work packages.
- Assign a business value to each item (between 1 and 10 where 10 is the highest business value).
- Assign a cost of delivery rating (between 1 and 5 where 1 is the costliest delivery and 5 is the cheapest).

▶

- Calculate the business value × cost of delivery and sequence the results in descending order.

- *Review and apply common sense!*

One of the great advantages of a Kanban board is how easy it is to shuffle the cards around during group discussion. This plays a vital part in agreeing the priorities once the to-do list shapes up. One of the cornerstones of Kanban is the business and delivery team working together in partnership – this is highly evident when all the interested parties are huddled around a board reviewing the priorities and asking *what's next then?*

Controlling Work-in-Progress (WiP)

In an ideal world each task plucked from the top of the *to-do* list progresses seamlessly to *job done* status before the next one is picked up. In reality life is never simple and most people end up with more than one thing on the go at any given time. This isn't multi-tasking, just switching effort whenever there's a temporary hold-up and this has been common practice from the year dot.

With Kanban there's an agreed limit to the total number of tasks in progress at any point in time – this is known as a *WiP limit*. It can be applied to individuals, the team collectively or both. A maximum of three things in progress per person is a popular individual ceiling. Or twice the number of team members as a maximum group threshold.

There's a tendency in certain circles to enjoy the early stages of any activity and for interest to wane towards the end, with a reluctance to tie up any loose ends. Kanban insures against this phenomenon with WiP limits. It helps avoid ending up with a sea of items *in progress* with many of them stuck at *99% complete*. As part of the *agile* philosophy, the *raison d'être* for work is achieving business value and that doesn't happen until the job is finished.

Imposing a WiP limit is critical for implementing Kanban successfully and as such it is non-negotiable. Without this in place the board can veer towards a glorified *to-do* list. With a WiP limit there's a continual flow of work getting through to genuine completion and paying dividends. Individuals are forced to confront blockers and deal with them rather than put jobs on the back burner with a defeatist shrug of the shoulders.

Continual process improvement is an important part of the Kanban method and for the most part it happens naturally. The WiP limit forces teams to be introspective when necessary and look at what's clogging up the production process. This creates a culture of being on the lookout for tweaks and adjustments that make the machine run more smoothly, literally in the case of the motor industry where it all started.

Kanban struggles with:

✗ Nothing much really if you think smart.

Managing projects with Kanban

At the very heart of *agile* is the concept of continuous delivery. No more long waits for anything of use to be delivered, as there's a continual flow of small, yet perfectly formed, packages. Kanban captures the very essence of this agile concept because every piece of work is a delivery in its own right. This becomes the ultimate litmus test for the perfect Kanban *user story*. Does it make sense in isolation? Will it put a smile on someone's face when it arrives on the doorstep?

Of course projects can be delivered using Kanban too. A project can be broken down into smaller packages or individual *user stories* to be delivered incrementally. Far from being unsuitable, Kanban encourages the business community to think smaller and ask for deliveries that provide a return in their own right yet are part of a bigger picture. Adding features to an established product is a great example.

 'A life spent at the edge of the pier is a life full of regret, a life full of fear.'

Ryan Lilly

The final word

One of the many great things about implementing Kanban is there's minimal disruption to the status quo. By using existing as-is workflows to begin with there's no risk of major disruption or losing things that are being done well. It's very much a case of evolution not revolution with no risk of throwing the baby out with the bathwater.

The changes are subtle and non-invasive yet are likely to have an immediate impact. Who in their right mind would argue against implementing a WiP limit? Once put into place, expect to see an immediate improvement in throughput with several light bulb moments along the way. There may be a few Doubting Thomases and Tinas to start with but results will turn them round.

Introducing a new, revolutionary process into an organisation is easier said than done. Selling _agile_ might seem very straight-forward after a couple of large glasses of wine yet turn out to be a tougher proposition when talking to colleagues who have heard it all before _and_ have their own agenda. There are people who get _agile_ immediately and are keen to climb on board but far more need nudging carefully in the right direction. The question is how?

Kanban is a great option to get a foot in the door. It's easy to understand and simple to launch. Even though it's a stress-free entry point for non-_agile_ organisations to test the water, Kanban isn't a compromise solution either. It can revolutionise teamwork and demonstrate what _agile_ can offer. Introducing Kanban is a solution in itself or it can be a step towards Scrum or whatever _agile_ framework tickles your corporate fancy.

One final cautionary note: Kanban is easy to understand and implement but easy enough to get wrong too. Don't be fooled into thinking it's _all so obvious_. Getting started is simple enough but getting the best out of Kanban is an acquired skill.

brilliant recap

- The Kanban _board_ is at the heart of the operation.
- Get started by visualising the as-is workflow.
- Limit the work-in-progress for maximum efficiency.
- Don't let the simplicity fool you; it's a deceptively powerful tool.
- Kanban can be a final destination... or a stepping stone for grander ambitions.

CHAPTER 5

Simply the best: Scrum essentials

Introduction

Scrum has become popular because it works. However, it hasn't been an overnight success – it's been on quite a journey to reach the incredible popularity it enjoys today. It had its roots in product development and innovation in mid-1980s Japan before being built on and refined in the US during the 1990s. People tried it, wrote papers on it, blogged about it but most crucially improved it by learning lessons. Eventually a critical mass of people delivered successful projects using it and the word was out.

Scrum now happily co-exists with a whole range of other *agile* frameworks and although they frequently snap at its heels for the No.1 spot, it remains the most popular primarily because it is just prescriptive enough to be helpful without drowning people and teams in burdensome rules, process and dogma. Moreover, it's one of the safest way to get started with for those new to the *agile* discipline because it has clearly defined roles and responsibilities, ceremonies and artefacts, yet allows enough flexibility in their implementation to let its customers feel supported but not suffocated.

Currently, Scrum is the most established method of *agile product delivery* there is, so there are plenty of options to help with it, from certified and non-certified training courses, to in-team coaching, one-to-one mentoring and a whole host of self-education options. Seasoned practitioners agree that Scrum is easy to do and hard to do well, so the key is to get a good grip of all the essentials required and start as you mean to go on.

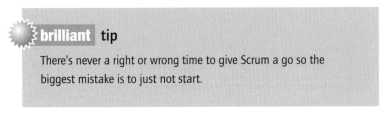

brilliant tip

There's never a right or wrong time to give Scrum a go so the biggest mistake is to just not start.

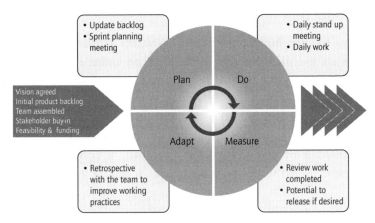

Figure 5.1 The Scrum framework

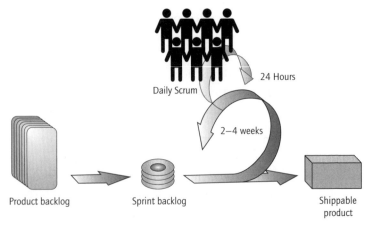

Figure 5.2 The sprint lifecycle

The Framework

Like all good ideas, Scrum is open to misunderstanding and misuse. To help make sure each implementation stays close to the original intent the creators, Ken Schwaber and Jeff Sutherland, created the much loved *Scrum Guide*. The guide is kept up to date and is freely available at **www.scrumguides.org** and it's seen as the single version of the truth. Changes are few and far between and at just 16 pages including a cover page and the table of contents, there's no excuse for failing to refer to it regularly.

 brilliant definitions

Scrum is a framework within which people can address complex adaptive problems, while productively and creatively delivering products of the highest possible value.

The Word according to Schwaber and Sutherland. We couldn't put it any better ourselves.

Scrum has always been about combining Lean and *agile* principles to help teams to deliver products. It isn't a project management tool, it's a framework for delivery and there's a subtle but important difference between the two. When Scrum is being done well it's a very natural process and it can be easy to forget it's even being used. Scrum is only there to *support* delivery – and we should always bear that in mind.

The end goal is to deliver good product using Scrum, not to try and get it working perfectly with delivery almost as an afterthought. It's there to serve and needs no glory, adulation or praise. It just helps us to get stuff done. However, we do need to let it do what it's good at, and to achieve this it isn't an option to pick and choose bits to use; it comes as a complete and perfectly formed package covering:

● **theory** – not much to get to grips with, just fundamental, guiding principles;

- **team roles** – only a Product Owner, the Scrum Master and the development team, yet all the essential bases are covered;
- **events** – the sprint itself, sprint planning at the start, the sprint review and the retrospective at the other end, with the infamous daily stand ups sandwiched in the middle:
- **artefacts** – the master product backlog, the sprint backlog and plenty of others beside.

'Don't be a time manager, be a priority manager.'

Denis Waitley

Self-organising teams

At the heart of Scrum is the concept of a self-organising team – a self-starting and self-governing team of experts that does whatever is needed to get the job done. The three roles within a Scrum team – Product Owner, Scrum Master and development team – are designed to make sure that everyone is able to work together seamlessly without stepping on each other's toes, yet not defined to such an extent as to make them inflexible and unable to adapt to change.

The Product Owner

First and foremost on the team sheet is the *Product Owner (PO)* who is the single, final decision maker for *what* the project is all about and *what* the end product delivers. They represent both the business sponsoring the product being built and the customers it's being built for. Strategically, the buck stops here.

When a business has an idea for a new product or service it will have to invest money and equally importantly *time* into developing it. The management team or strategists who run the business may well be happy to stump up the cash but they don't usually have the time to get as closely involved in guiding the

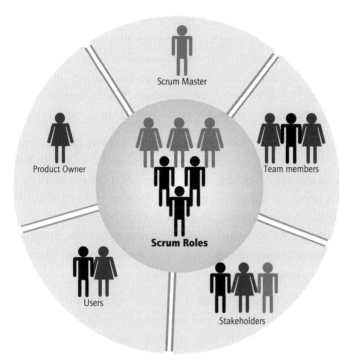

Figure 5.3 Scrum roles

product development as they would like. Leaving any project team to their own devices can be a recipe for disaster and it could also be seen as un-*agile*. So the smart move is to nominate a *business representative* and delegate day-to-day ownership of a product to them. This isn't a new idea in the project world but *agile* has made this role of Product Owner into an art form.

The Product Owner represents the business in all senses, managing the scope, scale and direction of the new project being built. It doesn't stop there either as they also represent the needs of the end customer too. Product Owners obsess about delivering value by representing the needs of the business *and* the end users, maximising the benefit delivered to both.

The business and the end customers are very different beasts. The business will have strong reasons for building something new and will be driven by a return on its investment of some description, perhaps straight financial profit or some other more noble reason. Although there can be multiple *business stakeholders*, they will almost certainly be outnumbered by the amount of end users planned for the new product. The challenge for the Product Owner is to represent both camps equally and fairly.

In this context the Product Owner is like a politician and walks a fine line. On one side they work within the boundaries of the law and deliver on policy, looking after the business's interests. This is usually a relatively small group or even just an individual. On the other side they also need to represent their many constituents. As they can't possibly meet all of them, they meet a representative sample and ultimately make decisions based on what they think is best for the majority.

The Product Owner is the final decision maker – although they can be lobbied by anyone and everyone to make decisions and priority calls, ultimately what they say goes. These decisions, for both the business and the end users, are made visible and accessible on the prioritised backlog – the tool the Product Owner uses to remain accountable when prioritising value.

Accountability is vital when turning this backlog into a working product. The team will have plenty of questions and the Product Owner will need to be available at all times to answer them to ensure the project keeps heading in the right direction and converging on the correct solution. Also from time to time the business will want reassuring that its money is being spent wisely and that its strategic objectives will be met.

This is by far the most challenging role and is a pivotal in a Scrum team. It looks easy enough on paper but requires a deft touch and a clear vision of where the business wants to go. Like Scrum itself, it's easy to do and easy to get badly wrong.

 **impact**

Good Product Owners obsess about delivering value by representing the needs of the business *and* the end users, maximising the benefit delivered to both.

At best the Product Owner is the guiding light for a Scrum team but when things go wrong it's usually the Product Owner that has led the team off on a merry dance.

The Scrum Master

The *Scrum Master* is the chief organiser on a project and they're often fondly described as a *servant-leader*, someone who shares power, puts the needs of others first and helps people develop and perform as highly as possible. This is in sharp contrast to a project manager who typically exerts top-down control. The Scrum Master is an enabler, helping a self-managing team to complete the task of delivering working, valuable product. One thing's for sure: organising a Scrum team isn't a walk in the park.

A Scrum Master facilitates all the ceremonies, making sure they happen on time, that the right people turn up, that the information to make the correct decisions is available and that the aims and outcomes are achieved. They need to be on tap to help the Product Owner manage the stakeholders if necessary and more than likely help keep the Product Owner on track. If that's not already enough, they're the guardians of *the process* making sure that things are done properly – like writing up proper user stories – and minimise distractions by managing any outside interaction with the team.

The Scrum Master is always oiling the wheels of progress. They sit with the team so that they can observe first-hand what's really going on, trying to find and remove impediments to progress. An extremely important part of this role is to coach the Product Owner, the team and even the wider organisation in *agile* best practice to make sure the job at hand is done efficiently. Key areas of focus are long-term product planning, effective and appropriate reporting plus acting on feedback in a timely way.

Whereas the Product Owner is the brain of the business, the Scrum Master has an equivalent status on the day-to-day operational side, creating the best possible environment for the team to operate within. The primary objective is to ensure the team can get on with the *real work*.

 **impact**

Scrum Masters are unsung, multitalented heroes: facilitators, enablers, occasional counsellors and regular crap cutters.
When on form, the Scrum Master makes the world a much easier place to live and work in.

The development team

In an *agile* environment *the development team* includes everyone else that's needed to get the job done. Their sole objective is to take the prioritised items off the backlog and turn them into working products. They're self-organising, which is a nice way of saying that they're trusted to work together as sensible grown-up professionals who can focus on getting work done properly without needing micro-management.

The development team is the project engine house. They're multi-talented, multi-disciplined and totally fixated on delivery. Crucial to the team ethos is the concept of being cross-skilled, which means that although it's relatively rare for someone to be able to do every single job required, the team members use their individual skills to help each other out in order to get the job done.

Ultimately, the development team must be self-motivated and dedicated to building the product as best they can. They're in total control of their own destinies because they manage themselves; no one will know how the team works better than the team themselves. The Product Owner owns the vision and the Scrum Master provides support wherever needed, but apart from that the team make their own minds up and only answer to themselves.

 **impact**

Whopping great teams are not efficient or effective. Communications, relationships and consequently bandwidth suffer when teams get too big. The *Scrum Guide* now advocates an optimal team size of six, plus or minus three although this recommendation has varied a little over the years. *Extensive research supports this advice so don't let the team size creep into double digits.*

Key Scrum events

Events in Scrum are simple, straightforward and always *time-boxed*. They're designed to give structure to the *inspect and adapt* ethos of the framework without constraining the participants to meaningless formality. Scrum needs all five events to be done in order to work properly; missing any of them out means you are not doing Scrum and leads to ineffective working practices, lack of visibility and confusion. Commonly, if teams are getting frustrated with a Scrum event and they have stopped finding it useful, it's a consequence of something else that's not being done properly.

The five Scrum events are:

✔ the sprint – provides a wrapper round the other events;

✔ sprint planning – happens at the very beginning;

✔ daily Scrum – occurs on a daily basis without exception;

✔ review – takes place at the end to showcase the outcomes;

✔ retrospective – wraps everything up nicely.

The sprint

A sprint is simply a time-box of between one and four weeks that provides a space for work to be done. Essentially, it's a container for all the other Scrum events. Typically teams choose two weeks as a good *sprint* length but there's no perfect duration and all have strengths and weaknesses. If in doubt, start with either a one or two week sprint and see how that pans out.

Sprints can be seen as an opportunity to run mini-projects, and provide the *regular heartbeat* of product development so don't be tempted to vary the duration of every other sprint. *Get into a groove.* A sprint starts with *planning* to decide what will be built in it and ends with a *review* of the product built. A *retrospective* for the team affords them space to assess how they have worked together and consider any applicable improvements.

brilliant timesaver

There's no mention of user stories in the *Scrum Guide* and there are many different ways for the Product Owner to describe what's required. User stories just happen to be, quite rightly, the most popular method.

Go with the in-crowd and don't waste time mulling over the other options.

Sprint Planning

Planning happens right at the start of each new sprint. It's an interactive session for the team to look at the user stories that the Product Owner has already refined, tuned and prioritised to see how many they think can be delivered within the time-box. There will be a frank and open discussion about complexities, risk, size, effort needed, business value and the details of what the business is asking for. The objective is for the team to fully comprehend and agree to what they're taking on.

A key characteristic of a Scrum planning session is that it's team led, albeit facilitated by the Scrum Master. In the old days a project manager would just *tell* the team what they have to get done and by when, whereas an *agile sprint planning* session lets the team decide what to take off the top of the prioritised backlog, allowing them to work at a realistic, sustainable rate. That's not to say they should set an easy target and the Scrum Master works with the team to ensure the end goal is challenging yet achievable. Ultimately the team have the final say when they have reached capacity.

The planning session is about confirming the understanding of each *product backlog item* before it's included in the sprint. It's essential that the business thinking be understood before work starts and any *serious* lack of clarity needs ironing out up front; that's what the Product Owner is there for. Resist the temptation to go into a session with a bunch of vague stories and promises, promises, promises.

Once the *user stories* that make up the sprint have been agreed then the Scrum Master and team get on with it! The thinking and pondering is over and the graft begins.

 **example**

The development team decide how much work to take into a sprint, as after all they'll be doing the work. but the Product Owner and the Scrum Master play their part too.

- Start with a clear sprint goal. Be clear about exactly what's wanted and how that goal will be measured.

- Select the highest priority user story. Check out the acceptance criteria and ensure everyone understands *what* it's about.

- Ask the team whether it can be completed this sprint. If the answer is yes and there are no serious concerns then it's in.

- If the answer is no then try to resolve the issue there and then. For example, by breaking down the story if it's too big, but if the answer is still no then out it goes.

- Repeat the process until the team eventually says *no way*. Sense check that the sprint backlog is challenging but doable.

- Get the Product Owner to confirm the sprint backlog meets the sprint goal. If it doesn't, work together collaboratively to rectify the problem.

- *Job done.*

Daily Scrum

The *daily Scrum* (or *daily stand-up* as it's often called elsewhere) is a time-boxed, micro-meeting that lasts no more than 15 minutes and occurs every day – preferably around a visual representation of current work. The more *in your face* this is, the better. The primary intent is to make sure the team members give each other a status check every 24 hours to ensure they're aligned to the goals set out in the planning session and on track to deliver the goods.

Sprints are mini-projects and like their big brothers they rarely go smoothly. Expect hiccups and use the daily Scrum to get blockers out in the open. This is where the Scrum Master gets down to business and picks up on any impediments that are obstructing progress with the expectation of facilitating a solution. This isn't

a case of lobbing problems over the fence but of sharing them with the expectation of getting a very big helping hand.

The daily Scrum follows a very simple format, asking each team member three questions:

- What did you do yesterday? *A progress update.*
- What will you do today? *Communicating intent.*
- What impediments do you have? *And this is the killer question.*

Just getting everyone to the daily Scrum on time and keeping them focused on the script is a job in itself. Any meeting can go wrong, even more so when it's on a very tight schedule and with a very sharp focus. A task for the Scrum Master is to make sure that the team isn't distracted from attending this meeting in the first place, that it occurs and that it stays focused and relevant to keeping the team on track. It might sound easy but it sure isn't and everybody plays their part in keeping things on track. The Scrum Master isn't a nursemaid and shouldn't contemplate sending deviants to the naughty corner. Well at least not literally.

The daily Scrum is a barometer indicating the health of the sprint itself, the effectiveness of the team and a pointer to a host of other things. An experienced observer, such as a trainer or coach, will only need to attend one or maybe two daily Scrums to offer an expert diagnosis on how things sit generally. Admittedly even in a mature environment these sessions rarely go totally smoothly but a dysfunctional stand-up is an extremely serious warning signal, *especially* when it's not a one-off blip.

brilliant example

Vigilance is needed to keep the daily Scrum on track. Ultimately this is all about the people involved and there are certain personality traits that are capable of causing a serious derailment:

- **Noisy observer:** who is not part of the team but will try and butt in and cause disruption. Get the Scrum Master to explain that observers are there to observe only! Their comments can be made offline.
- **Late arriver:** who arrives for the meeting late and then asks to hear what everyone has just said again. Don't backtrack unless absolutely necessary as it only encourages this bad habit.
- **Side-tracker:** disrupts the meeting, often unintentionally, but always with negative consequences. The corrective advice offered is to stick to the script and update the team efficiently; we can hear all about your bad date another time.
- **Habitual hater:** doesn't want to be there and is uncooperative as a result. Well tough luck, so shape up or ship out because everyone in the team has to play by the rules.
- **Silent types:** even if someone is a bit shy they've got to chip in. The non-negotiable rule is that everybody contributes and silence isn't golden.
- **Futurists:** trying to star gaze into the future instead of focusing on the here and now is a distraction. Leave the vision to the Product Owner and concentrate on the next delivery.
- **Problem solver:** anyone who wants to spend the daily stand-up solving others' problems. Encourage problem sharing but save the resolution until after the meeting so it doesn't distract others.

Keep on the lookout for offenders, especially anyone who is guilty on several counts. And *know thyself* in case the main culprit is close to home.

The Review

A product review, more commonly known simply as a *review*, is the opportunity for the team to show the fruits of their labours to the Product Owner. There are many opinions out there about what this should entail but in essence it's just a way to get vital feedback on *what* they're doing. The feedback serves a number of purposes:

- **Facilitating pre-release product scrutiny:** letting the team know whether what they're building is fundamentally right or wrong

- **Reviewing strategic objectives:** checking the sprint goals are going to be met, with an opportunity to address any concerns.

- **Massaging stakeholder expectations:** this is at all levels and at an early stage; *what they see is what they'll get!* No last-minute surprises.

There are those who are adamant that at the end of the sprint, user stories should have been turned into working, tested, potentially usable product and this is both correct and admirable. But even if that isn't always the case, the Product Owner should review everything anyway. Honesty is the best policy and it's better to be open about a failed delivery and any problems encountered. At the very least it's an opportunity to review work-in-progress.

---

brilliant example

The Review is open to all *within reason*. This is when the team, supported by the Scrum Master, deliver the work they agreed to do during the sprint planning. *The proof is in the pudding.* All interested parties, end users and stakeholders should be at this session too, but mainly just to observe not to participate.

Pay adequate attention to the logistics. Secure a suitable room well in advance and any equipment needed to execute the demonstration. Set up ▶

in advance and prepare the presentation without over-rehearsing. There's nothing worse in the Scrum world than undermining two weeks of hard graft with a botched demo.

Keep to a simple format, put the session into context and don't just launch into the detail. Pretend your old impatient Aunt Rose is there and keep things light yet professional. Don't spin out material: there's nothing wrong with being in and out in 15 minutes:

- The Scrum Master introduces the team, sets the scene and reconfirms the agreed sprint goal.
- All cards are put on the table up front, with the Scrum Master stating whether everything was completed and if not, why not.
- The Scrum Master restates the user stories taken into the sprint.
- Each User Story is demonstrated. The team member who led its development shows it to the group. Afterwards, the Product Owner is asked for feedback.
- Anything else of relevance is highlighted, including minor features worthy of a mention or related issues.
- The Scrum Master gives the Product Owner a final chance to comment or make suggestions before deciding whether they're happy to accept the work package.
- Other attendees are given an opportunity to offer their tuppence worth.
- The Scrum Master confirms when the next review will happen, formally closes the session and if all went according to plan, breathes a sigh of relief.

Retrospectives

At the end of each sprint, once the review is over and the Product Owner and stakeholders have gone on their merry way, the team gets together to reflect on how things panned out. This is called a *retrospective* and it takes place without fail, even if everything went exactly according to plan. There's just as much to be learned from good execution as there is from a debacle. Don't *ever* be tempted to assume it's going to be a waste of time and rush headfirst into the next sprint.

Without wishing to sound like a broken record, this sounds easy to do, yet is challenging to do well. The core intent behind the retrospective is to bring the team together to talk about themselves, how they work, interact and deliver. This is by far the best possible illustration of the *agile* concept of *inspect and adapt*, looking at how the team worked together as a team and trying to find ways to make improvements. It's the cornerstone of being a self-managing, self-organising team and must be taken seriously. It is as non-negotiable as any of the other Scrum events but the most likely to be considered unnecessary. Don't commit that rookie error.

 'Always focus on the front windshield and not the rear-view mirror.'

Colin Powell

The outcome of the retrospective is a set of tangible and specific actions that helps the team improve their ability to deliver quality product. There's no need to generate reams and reams of ideas; a few well-chosen recommendations are far more likely to be implemented than a shedload of half-baked, hugely speculative ideas. Put a ceiling of five in place to maximise the chances of success.

brilliant example

Retrospectives are best kept tight and structured. Gather the team into a room with plenty of sticky notes, marker pens and a board set up as below. Ask the attendees to write as many things as they can think of about how they have fared over the last sprint. Good practice is to devote each sticky note to one point and to read each one out as they're put onto the board. ▶

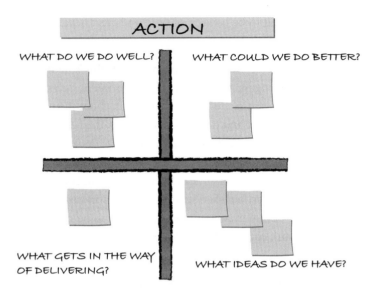

Once the team runs out of things to add, get everyone to look out for common themes. Group sticky notes together and give them a clear, descriptive title.

Discuss the themes and order them in terms of importance or severity and then assign clear actions for each, owned by one team member, to get them resolved. The person who owns an action doesn't have to resolve the issue but is responsible for making sure it *does* get resolved. There's little point investing time in a retrospective if there are no tangible *results*.

As there will be a retrospective every sprint, don't generate too many actions. One or two biggies or five smaller ones are perfect.

Scrum artefacts

Scrum artefacts are the items needed by the team to succeed. The non-negotiable big three are: the product backlog, the sprint backlog and the sprint burn down. Others are worth checking out down the line but stick to the essentials until they're properly mastered. In fact, many practitioners don't ever feel the need to travel further afield.

Product backlog

The *product backlog* is a shopping list of ideas needed to deliver the end product: a list of *desirements* if you will. This backlog

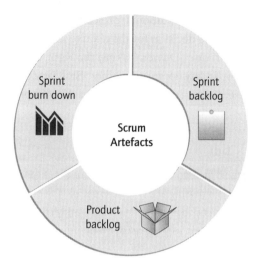

Figure 5.4 Scrum artefacts

ensures the Product Owner's agenda is transparent, visible and easily accessible. It includes everything that might need to be done, not only the specific tangible stuff but all the non-functional things too.

The backlog is owned and often jealously guarded by the Product Owner who remains accountable for it at all times. Of course they will, quite rightly, be canvassed, influenced and *occasionally* persuaded to reconsider the priority of the entries on an on-going basis. In fact the product backlog must be a living document, changing and developing all the time, with items getting added or removed as the product develops and more is learned about it.

Sprint backlog

Within every sprint the team needs a clear plan of what's going to be worked on. The Product Owner prioritises the product backlog but the workers need to decide how many of the highest priority items can go into the sprint. The *sprint backlog* is a prioritised list of those items and is what the team agrees can be done in that time-box. Unlike traditional projects, how much the team take into a sprint is a decision for the team to make, not the Scrum Master or the Product Owner. Taking the right amount of work in to the sprint is key to sustainability. Best practice, based on common sense, is to work on the sprint backlog in priority order.

brilliant tip

A static product backlog is a sure-fire indicator of a project in trouble; change is healthy and is to be expected. The opposite applies to sprint backlogs and if they're constantly churning once in play there's something very iffy going down.

Sprint burn down

One of Scrum's key strengths is the way metrics are embraced and used to great effect. Gone are the days of speculating about progress or of getting stuck at *nearly complete* status. The *sprint burn down* chart is a simple visual representation of progress and the team uses it to track the product development effort remaining in a sprint.

brilliant tip

When updating the work remaining in a sprint, only deduct the story points of genuinely *completed* tasks to reflect real progress. Don't factor in anything that is allegedly 25%, 50% or 75% finished.

Be especially wary of anything reported as 99% complete.

The final word

Going *agile* is similar to learning to drive. It looks very easy when you're sitting in the passenger seat and it is *pretty* straightforward once you've grasped the basics. But only a lunatic would jump into the driver's seat and zoom off on an important mission on the basis of reading a couple of interesting articles on the internet. At the very least any right-minded person gets properly to grips with the theory. Think of this material as the equivalent of getting stuck into the *Highway Code* but hopefully just a touch lighter.

A basic understanding of the Scrum framework is essential before jumping in. Not just understanding the basic concepts but think also about getting to grips with how it all hangs together so perfectly. Now there are many examples of so-called Scrum teams operating with key roles missing, using a subset of ceremonies and selected artefacts; some even achieve results after a fashion. But the fact is that for sustained success it's necessary to have a thorough grounding in Scrum theory before heading off. Don't forget: inexperienced drivers are the number one cause of serious car crashes.

brilliant recap

- Scrum is popular because it works. Don't fall into the trap of thinking that bits can be missed out and it will still yield results.

- Have a clear vision and backlog; ensure there's only one Product Owner making decisions about the content and prioritisation.

- Deliver work with *business* value in every sprint. Working, usable product is the only sign of success.

- Develop working practices, requirements, acceptance criteria, processes - everything as a team - with representatives of all the different disciplines.

- Don't put the product development team under too much pressure. Teams that work at a sustainable rate deliver better than those who are continually stressed.

- The best way to start is to, well, just start!

CHAPTER 6

Going on a journey: Scrum day by day

Introduction

Scrum is a great tool but it's just that – a tool. Very interesting to look at and check over but only comes into its own when used in anger. Like all tools, especially the best ones, the more you use it the defter and more expert you become. *Practice makes perfect,* which is handy because Scrum is founded on a repetitive cycle purposely designed to ensure doing the same useful tasks until they're second nature.

Perfection is the enemy of progress, so no need to plan your Scrum implementation to the *n*th degree before heading off. It's far better to *inspect and adapt* and implement incremental improvements along the way. There may even be big things that are obviously not quite right early on and need changing immediately. Perhaps the team location isn't quite right or anti-Scrum whingers are creating too much turbulence. Over time the bigger issues will be resolved and get replaced by a regular flow of smaller, much more manageable fixes.

If you're not making changes, not making advances no matter how small, then you're missing the point. Sometimes the desire to change subsides, resulting with an acceptance of the malfunctioning status quo. Occasionally a fear of rocking the boat prevents even minor adjustments. Sometimes, almost incredibly, there's a belief that things are pretty much perfect as they are!

Get to grips with the Scrum cycle of life but never become complacent or accepting. In one sense the set steps along the way are highly predictable and unvarying but in a much more important way they are never exactly the same twice.

'Do, or do not. There is no try.'

Yoda

Getting ready to roll

More often than not people who don't understand *agile* ways of working believe there's no planning involved. Not only is this nonsense for *agile* frameworks generally, it's particularly unfair where Scrum is concerned. Planning is, quite rightly, considered to be of paramount importance and it isn't a one-off set piece, more a case of *little and often*. The Scrum Master and the Product Owner are at their most effective when conversations are taking place all the time about what needs to be done and what is or isn't possible.

These discussions are all centred on the *product backlog*. This is the most important artefact that any project has, truly the backbone of proceedings. Frequently, the quality of the backlog will reflect the health of the project and vice versa. Even the best team in town will struggle to achieve anything without a decent backlog and it's constantly being reviewed and fine-tuned to make sure it's in excellent shape.

brilliant tip

Ninety-nine out of 100 new Scrum teams start their first ever sprint on an overly optimistic note and are light on preparation. User stories aren't quite there or scenarios aren't fully formed or lack acceptance criteria. Or even all three! Nine out of 10 of those teams repeat the same mistake in their second sprint.

Buck the trend.

Backlog refinement

Backlog refinement was previously known as *backlog grooming* but was rebadged for obvious reasons. Many less politically correct diehards still use the original moniker and whatever the preferred name it's the on-going practice of keeping the backlog in good shape and in priority order. In other words, prioritised by value or benefit by the business or end user.

The final decision for the priority order stays with the Product Owner and to some extent beauty is in the eye of the beholder, so it isn't an exact science. Don't get hung up on getting the sequence perfect. What's more important is getting the business requirements – the user stories, for example – in damn good shape. Backlog refinement meetings to prepare stories for the sprint should be scheduled regularly and ideally include at least one person from each *discipline* in the team.

There are teams that look at the backlog on a daily basis and others that are more *laissez-faire*. Zero refinement is a recipe for disaster and without doubt leads to messy sprints. A bigger investment up front pays dividends but there is a balance to be struck. By the time the sprint starts it should be just about the mechanics of execution, not about what the business wants and whether it's doable. By then the user stories should be good to go.

brilliant tip

The Product Owner is responsible for the quality of the user stories and accountable for the state of the backlog. If they do their job properly then sprint planning will run smoothly. If not, the planning will be repeatedly sidetracked by requests for clarification.

Acceptance criteria

The quickest way to get the development team to build the wrong thing is if they don't quite understand the requirements to begin with. Outright misunderstandings are the biggest issue but are usually easy to weed out during the refinement sessions; however, with *agile*, like many other frameworks, the real devil is in the detail. Subtle misunderstandings that come to light late on have an accumulated impact and occur more frequently than outright disasters.

The simplest way to avoid this is by pinning down collaboratively the acceptance criteria in advance; to establish a joint understanding of exactly how the Product Owner will judge the delivery to be a success. This must be understood at a macro level for the sprint itself of course but also for each and every requirement (e.g. every user story).

The best way to sort this out is actually for the team to co-author the *acceptance criteria*. There are many ways to do this but whenever stuck try answering the question: *I know I will have got <whatever> when <something happens>*. The *whatever* clause is a tangible delivery and the *something happens* can be a positive or negative experience. Think of this as anticipating what the Product Owner will articulate when the actual delivery is really made. Start with the end in mind.

Types of acceptance criteria include:

- a simple description of the outcome expected;
- bullet points;
- conditions of satisfaction;
- *Gherkin* language style using the Given, When, Then format.

 **example**

It's very tempting to start sprints on an optimistic note and vow to play catch-up later, particularly when the first ever sprint is about to begin and enthusiasm gets the better of common sense. Of course it's hard to be a ▶

party-pooper when all the rah-rah is going on, so even the people who know better cross their fingers and hope for the best. Then the inevitable happens and it's just a case of how bad the fallout is.

There are teams who get off on the wrong foot and never recover. The first failed delivery can fatally undermine confidence, especially when expectations are running high. Getting off to such a bad start makes it difficult to do the right thing on the second sprint and then there's a risk of a negative spiral. It's inevitable that there will be some problems early on – this is a pretty big step after all – so don't increase the risk levels by ignoring basic good practice.

Prioritisation in action

When prioritising there's no need to get hung up on the detail. It isn't like the Olympics where the difference between first, second and third can be life changing and fourth can mean it's been a wasted journey. It doesn't matter whether a user story is first on the list when the sprint starts or sneaks in by the skin of its teeth; all that matters is: *in* or *out*? Or more accurately, whether it is delivered or not delivered.

As sprints are relatively short, it's very much like waiting for a bus. *Another one will be along soon.* This reduces the pressure considerably and there's no need to agonise endlessly over priorities. The Product Owner only has to wait for another two weeks – or whatever the agreed standard length of a sprint is – before another delivery turns up. No need to panic.

 'Perfect is the enemy of good.'

Voltaire

Estimating in action

It's essential that every item in the backlog that has a reasonable chance of making it into the next sprint is given an estimate up front, preferably properly understood and sized but at the very least with a decent approximation. The biggest worry is when estimates just can't be agreed for one or more reasons. It's bad enough when teams take a bit of a punt on what they can deliver in a sprint, but if it's impossible to come up with a guesstimate it can point to a far more problematic underlying issue:

- **Poorly defined requirements:** vague user stories are hard to estimate, and guess what, they're even harder to deliver. *Get more detail in there.*

- **Too big and complex:** if a piece of work is more than a few days, delivery becomes a guessing game. *Break them down!* Big requirements carry more risk, as they are less understood.

- **Inadequate acceptance criteria:** if the destination isn't clear it becomes hard to gauge how long it will take to get there. Even with clear acceptance criteria, some might think that a piece of work is huge while others think it's tiny.

Estimation must be a collective effort. Once again let's put on the broken record and comment that, like many other *agile* activities, it's the conversation that's important. A diverse group of people discussing a subject will help approach it from all angles, demystify it and pin down what it takes to deliver. The process is not aiming for perfection; in fact teams that get into that frame of mind start hitting different problems: a broad brushstroke works fine and dandy.

Our recommendation is to go for *T-shirt sizing* or, even better, *story pointing* but we concede newbie teams find it easier to go for old-fashioned minutes, hours and days. Our experience is that once newish Scrum teams get into the groove they graduate away from *actual* measures and head for one of the *relative* approaches.

 example

	Pros	Risks
T-shirt sizing Small, medium or large	Quick, easy, understood by all	Can be too vague especially if XL and XXL are necessary
Story points A relative measure of complexity and effort	The relative sizing maintains integrity no matter what the skill-set of those actually doing the work	Can be tempting to have a fixed exchange rate into time and undermine the intent
Time Estimating the time it will take to do something	Easy to explain and universally understood	All of the shortcomings of old-style task estimating

Before diving into the sprint there's no need for an extensive pre-flight check and there are only three non-negotiable pre-conditions for a safe take-off:

1 Backlog is in priority order and agreed with the Product Owner.

2 Acceptance criteria are written in conjunction with the team or at least some of them.

3 Estimates exist for all the stories that will be coming next.

 definition

The best range of numbers to choose from during story point is based on the *Fibonacci sequence*: 0, 1, 2, 3, 5, 8, 13, 21, 34, 55, 100..... Anything at the lower end of the scale is a small piece of work right through to a massive top end. This scale works brilliantly with many Scrum estimating techniques especially *Planning Poker*.

Anything that's too hot to handle should be 100. A 55 rings alarm bells and even a 34 has a warning attached.

Starting the sprint

When the sprint starts, the first item on the agenda is *sprint planning*. Frequently referred to simply as *planning* by teams, this is distinct from *release planning* and hugely different to *project planning*. Sprint planning is a pivotal and therefore mandatory for the whole team to attend. This is where the sprint should get off on the right foot but can be where it all starts to unravel.

The objective is for the team to confirm what it will take in to the sprint with a view to delivering it back to the Product Owner as working product. When the preparation is inadequate, then make sure the planning session incorporates the final *grooming* and *refinement* that should have taken place up front. This isn't ideal of course but it does happen and it's a much better option than building a sprint semi-blindly and hoping for the best.

brilliant timesaver

There are plenty of quick and easy ways to spot it's all going pear-shaped:

- No one knows what work is coming next.
- The same retrospective actions keep coming up.
- It's quiet and the team aren't talking to each other.
- There's a lack of trust between certain individuals.
- A lack of transparency and basic information are apparent.
- It's way too stressful and tempers are frayed.
- The Product Owner has gone AWOL.
- *The team aren't delivering!*

Get the mechanics right

If the preparation has been comprehensive with the proper completion of user stories, acceptance criteria and story pointing, then planning ends up being just a session where the development team confirms it understands what the Product Owner wants and agrees how much the team can deliver back at the end of the sprint. That's the way it should be with the focus exclusively on *what* and nothing more; thus getting the mechanics right is all that matters:

- **Logistics.** One of the main tasks for the Scrum Master during planning is, of course, to facilitate the session. But an equally important job is to sort out the logistics in advance. There's more to this than meets the eye and includes booking a room, inviting the Product Owner and the team, making sure the user stories are ready along with a suitable sprint goal and, on an associated note, to ensure the Product Owner is fully prepared. During the session itself the Scrum Master is there solely to make sure the outcome is reached.

- **Duration.** A planning session is a great opportunity for focused discussion about specifics and will need adequate space. But realistically it's not possible to maintain a high intensity for hours and hours on end, so be pragmatic and limit the gathering to a couple of hours max. If time gets called before the team reach their absolute sprint capacity, don't worry too much as they can always pull in other stories later on. In fact, during the early days it's better to leave a bit of wiggle room and subsequently add work in rather than overcommit and fail to meet the planned target.

- **Outcome.** The objective of sprint planning is that the team and the Product Owner agree on *what* will be delivered at the end of the sprint; this is primarily about setting and managing expectations. Invariably the Product Owner will want more work to be done than the team can possibly do. So the team need to know their capacity and only take in the amount of work that they feel they can do to progress at a sustainable pace. This can be a little hit-and-miss for the first few attempts – yet another reason to err on the side of caution.

Avoid personal issues

Getting the preparation right and keeping a close watch on the mechanics is a great start but the biggest risk of derailment is from *people problems*. Planning is all about the interaction between the participants, so there's plenty that can and *will* go wrong:

- **Disengagement.** Planning should be quick, engaging and motivating. Generally, if a team finds planning boring and tunes out it means they're either not finding it relevant or don't feel involved. There are several possible causes including simply a lack of clarity about what's required from them to telling the team what to do instead of letting them apply their own expertise and intelligence.

- **Arguments.** Healthy debate is to be encouraged but arguments are counterproductive and hugely distracting. The Product Owner is the key decision maker and the best person to make a decision to help move the team forwards.

- **Frustration.** Let the team be heard as it's mind bogglingly frustrating and counterproductive to be ignored! They do the work, they're the key problem solvers and integral to delivering a working product – without them nothing will be delivered. So if *anyone* makes a point, sit up and listen.

- **Solutionising.** If a development team starts to drill down in too much detail in a planning session, chances are they're probably trying to figure out the solution. A planning session is there to agree *what* the team can deliver at the end of the sprint. The detail of *how* the tasks are done can be left until later on.

- **Pressure.** The team must never be pressured into taking on more work than they feel capable of doing. It never ends well. They decide for themselves how much work they need to take on to work at a sustainable pace. This is sacred and needs to be protected; the team will fail to deliver if it's a one-off or just burn out over time if it happens regularly.

Planning good practice

The Scrum Master is the master of ceremonies during sprint planning and responsible for facilitating the session but there's a joint responsibility around maintaining good practice. The Scrum Master should prevent any slippage into bad habits but if this does happen the team must pipe up too. Keeping things on track is a collaborative effort:

- Never start planning without the Product Owner and representatives from all the key disciplines.

- Resist the temptation to accept badly written or ill-prepared user stories as-is with a view to patching them up later.

- Don't attempt a massive rescue job by interpreting the stories, doing the story pointing and writing the acceptance criteria on the fly.

- Be sure issues and problems are resolved properly before moving on; sometimes the Product Owner and the team just need time.

- If stalemate is reached, take action. Keep up the pace. Move to the next item and then come back to the initial issue later.

- Don't let anyone, *especially* the Scrum Master, tell the team what to do and dictate their conclusions.

---

brilliant example

A Scrum team delivered a new electronic tool for managing corporate data and the Product Owner requested an enhancement. During sprint planning the lead IT developer estimated it was only about 10 minutes work. Even though the sprint was pretty full the team were happy to slot in such a small change.

When it came to picking up the work, the software testers pointed out that the modification was at the heart of several complex processes. It took days to iron out all the issues and complete all of their checks. During the planning session nobody from the test team had been available.

The small change wasn't delivered in the sprint and two other highly desirable features were also affected. The lack of test team input meant a decision had been based on incomplete information. Consequently, despite valiant efforts, the delivery fell short.

The Product Owner was gutted but the whole team learnt a very valuable lesson: without reps from all the disciplines, planning becomes a case of finger crossing.

Days in the middle

Once planning is completed, it's time for the team to crack on with the hard graft. From their point of view what happens here very much depends on the nature of the project. The main thing is for the team to deliver whatever they've planned and agreed. The Scrum Master plays a pivotal part in helping them out during these key days in the middle of the sprint by:

- **Keeping up momentum.** Often it's the basics that get overlooked and cause the biggest problems. Is everyone clear about what they need to do? Do team members need any extra information from either outside or inside the team? Are there any dependencies, are they waiting on others? Even experienced team members can need encouragement to speak up and highlight their issues. The Scrum Master must be proactive and persistent.

- **Removing impediments.** This is the most widely advertised part of the Scrum Master's role and the number one question at the daily Scrum is: *do you have any impediments?* This is about doing whatever it takes to keep things moving. Tasks can come in every form, from plugging in cables under desks to helping the Product Owner report back to senior stakeholders.

- **Keeping information flowing.** A two-way exchange both into and out of the team. From the team will come any *dependencies, impediments* and of course *progress reports*. The team will expect time with the Product Owner to get questions answered and for a clear and visible backlog to be maintained. Facilitating all this, producing metrics and dealing with people is time-consuming and can be tricky. It's a full-time job.

- **Tracking progress.** Burn down and burn up charts are the two most useful reports to track and communicate as the project progress. A *burn down chart* shows how much work remains to be done whereas a *burn up chart* shows how much work has been completed so far. We recommend following the *agile* crowd by *at least* producing a burn down chart every day.

 **example**

The most widely used mechanism for reporting sprint progress is the burn down chart. It plots the work remaining in the sprint against a target *burn down rate*. There are two lines on the chart:

1   work outstanding – over time;

2   target *burn down* – over time.

It starts with the burn down rate required to complete all of the work on time. In the example below the dotted line plots the story points in the sprint over its duration – starting with the total number, down to zero at the end. This is the benchmark that progress can be judged against. Simplistically, if progress is above the line, then the team are behind and anything below the line indicates the team are ahead of the game.

The dashed line plots the total amount of work outstanding each day. As each task is completed, the story points (or whatever unit of measure is used) are deducted and the results get plotted accordingly. There are times when tasks are not completed on a given day and this creates a stairs effect rather than a smooth decline.

In our example we see that the team falls a bit behind early on but then step up a gear to finish on time. It's not unusual for progress to deviate from the target, but anything significant is either an early warning of things going very well or extremely badly.

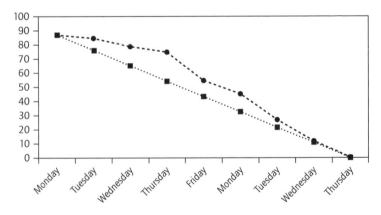

Figure 6.1 Brilliant burn down

- **Preparing for the next sprint.** Is the backlog being continually reviewed and refined? Are the user stories well written and visible? Are the necessary rooms booked for the next round of planning and have the right people been invited? Are all the other logistics under control? Nothing onerous but the arrangements need constant attention to avoid last-minute glitches. Always think well ahead.

brilliant tip

If there's any possibility of bad news at the end of a sprint, not completing all the work for example, then the Product Owner needs to know early on so expectations can be managed. There are always politics to be considered.

Getting near the end

The end of the *sprint* is never far away and it pays to plan ahead. The Scrum Master must get everything ready for the product review, the team retrospective and of course the next sprint planning session. Apart from thinking about how to play the meetings themselves, the logistics need to be sorted out. Getting everyone in the right place at the right time is easier said than done.

brilliant tip

Forward plan and block book all of the Scrum ceremonies especially the outward-facing sprint review. Keep to the same day of the week *and* the same time. Get everyone into a regular heartbeat and don't change the arrangements unless there are exceptional circumstances.

Same day, same time, same place is a brilliant sprint habit.

One thing is for sure: nothing ever quite goes according to plan. No one can see into the future and it's impossible to anticipate everything that might disrupt the sprint plan. From unexpected sick leave to contagious computer viruses, there's no such thing as a cast-iron road map. The end of the sprint is about delivering what was agreed to back to the Product Owner, with the express intent to get feedback. Teams should naturally feel that they *want* to meet the expectations set at the start even if it means having to put in a little extra effort just to cross the line.

A day or two before the end of the sprint is the time for the Scrum Master to be on high alert and actively seeking out anything that needs to be addressed in order to get the sprint closed. The best time to air issues and get help is during the daily Scrum. It's a great place to spot festering problems and nip them in the bud. The normal body language rules apply so look out for anyone looking nervous or trying to avoid eye contact. Ask probing questions and remember that the Scrum Master is the chief organiser whose job it is to help the development team deliver back to the Product Owner.

End of the sprint

If all the work doesn't get finished, it's bad news but not the end of the world. Of course, it's important to find out why and try to avoid the problem the next time; that's all part of the *agile* philosophy of *inspect* and *adapt*. And of course there's a big difference between reasons we have no control over, like illness, and things we do, like taking too much work into a sprint. Any user stories that aren't completed can be flipped into the next sprint but be careful not to underestimate the work outstanding. Generally it's best to consider them as *not-started* to avoid confusion or problems with estimating part stories.

 **tip**

At the end of each sprint, the total number of story points in the user stories delivered by the team is their *velocity*. Over time, the average *velocity* stabilises and becomes more reliable.

The team can use this as a guide for how much can be accepted into the next sprint.

At the end of the sprint *you are where you are.* By then an accomplished Scrum Master and experienced team members will have already thought about what has been going on in the sprint and made notes about what was good and bad as well as points to be addressed next time. Taking notes needn't be physical and there's no need to walk around with a clipboard doing time-and-motion studies on people.

Learning lessons is a vital part of the *agile* process and the best Scrum teams are continually *inspecting* and *adapting* their working practices. Making mental notes is more than enough and team dynamics are usually rich pickings. How are people interacting in the daily Scrum? How do they talk to one another and what is the banter like where the team sits? Who's acting like they don't care and who's on fire? What about the inter-personal dynamics, the gossip and the opinions that are being stated?

Minds need to turn to managing the message coming out of the team about what has been accomplished. Regardless of *what* has been delivered (or not, as might be the case), there will always be comments and enquiries – sometimes things can get quite heated as tricky questions are asked about what has been delivered and team performance. The best thing to do is paint a realistic but positive picture of how things have gone. Tell the story of the sprint and why you ended up where you did.

Closing the sprint is usually the busiest and most stressful time for the Scrum Master and the team. Tensions run high and expectations need to be met. There's still plenty to cover off especially with the *sprint review, sprint retrospective* and *sprint planning* about to happen. It's important for the team to stick together at this point even if their backs are up against the wall. Keep your shape and be methodical; don't be political, be functional. Be calm. Be patient. It will all be fine.

brilliant example

An inexperienced Scrum Master had to stand up in front of about 30 people at a sprint review, some of them very senior in the organisation, and tell them that in the latest three-week sprint the team hadn't completed even one solitary user story. The Scrum Master looked pretty pasty after a sleepless night and seemed very uncomfortable when it was time to spill the beans.

The Scrum Master was open about not achieving anything and explained that the team understood why it had happened and what it was going to do about it. The strangest thing happened. The Scrum Master and the team received praise across the board. It turns out that people there appreciated their honesty and the fact that there was a *cunning plan*. Moreover support was offered from a variety of sources to help get things fixed.

Things don't always go swimmingly, even on a Scrum project. Honesty is the best policy and is always respected. It's more important to have a plan to address the issues than have carefully honed excuses.

The final word

If the Scrum Master and the Product Owner are looking pretty relaxed at the end of the sprint, then things are going pretty well. Regular peace and calm is the Holy Grail of Scrum: much sought after but unlikely to be found. When Scrum works well it looks easy. In reality though there's no such thing as perfection. There's no wrong way or right way to do Scrum but always a *better* way. Never give up looking for improvements even when things are going brilliantly.

Scrum teams are judged by results but there other positive signs to look out for. A great rapport between the Product Owner and the team is one of them. A team that's self-managing and making good, clear decisions is another. It's also telling when senior managers, stakeholders and end users like what's going on and the product road map is clear. So when good working product is delivered time and time again and the retrospectives bring up smaller and less important issues to resolve, what more can possibly be asked for? Then the only risk is complacency or boredom setting in.

The Scrum ethos is about continuous improvement. At the start of a Scrum project the improvements can be huge in size and many in number. At times it can feel like an overwhelming challenge but it's also engaging and even *fun* sometimes. Paradoxically, Scrum can also become the constraint. Teams can get to the stage where the framework around Scrum is holding them back. That's a very nice problem to have and only a few end up there! For the majority of us the key is to keep trying new things. Never stop trying to improve.

Practice make *nearly perfect*.

 recap

- Set the bar high. Continually refine the backlog, develop good acceptance criteria and use only well-written user stories in sprints.

- The Scrum Master helps make things happen, organises the team, develops good practice and removes impediments.

- Good metrics help support informed decisions *and* provide great reporting.

- The team is expert at problem solving so let them get on with their job without interference.

- Learn lessons and always think ahead; Scrum never sleeps.

CHAPTER 7

Agile in the organisation

Introduction

One of the biggest reasons for projects failing is because they end up detached from the real world and tangible business needs. There are many reasons why this happens but the ultimate outcome is always *customer dissatisfaction* and the only variable is the degree of customer unhappiness. A big selling point for *agile* is that this just cannot happen. The whole *agile* ethos is built on collaboration and involvement. The business team is involved in every step and every important decision along the way.

Many frameworks treat maintaining this type of business buy-in and involvement as an important objective but with *agile* it's a non-negotiable part of the process. The difference is that this active participation is a foundation stone for *agile*, not an optional add-on. Gaining the initial support and buy-in to launch *agile* is the biggest ask but sustaining that support is vital for success. It's true that once adopted and bedded in, *agile* can look after itself and growth is organic from then on, but there's much to be done to reach that self-sustaining situation.

A big bang launch isn't essential and the first step can be a small one. But winning the hearts and minds of the right people is vital to get off to a solid start. Understanding what people in the organisation want, what their problems are and how *agile* can help them is an important part of the process. The end game isn't an isolated *agile* experiment – even though a one-off project will provide a handsome return – an internal *agile* revolution is the potential corporate game changer. That final goal is very achievable but it will require plenty of help and support along the way.

The wider and more diverse the belief in *agile* is, the better. Part of the strategy for getting *agile* out there is to win over all the key players, to win over the organisation. What's in it for them? Plenty!

> It is wise to persuade people to do things and make them think it was their own idea.

Nelson Mandela

Reasons to go *agile*

There's a host of *personal* reasons for being interested in *agile*, ranging from a desire to find better ways to do things through to unabashed self-interest. There are many *agilists* on a private crusade to convert the business world and just as many who see it as a damn good career move. It doesn't really matter too much as the move will be a genuine win–win situation whatever the primary motive.

Layered on top of personal drivers are plenty of hard-nosed business reasons for wanting to adopt *agile*. These aren't vague, aspirational desires such as *improving customer satisfaction* or *becoming a world-class organisation* or *creating an innovative environment* – honourable though they all are – these are drivers that are specific and measurable. Business objectives from introducing *agile* need to be smart or more accurately *SMART*.

The real killer argument that wins over the seen-it-all-before doubters is that *agile* delivers results within months, more often weeks – everybody from the management team through to the people doing the *real work*.

🔘 **brilliant** definition

SMART objectives are:
S – specific, significant, stretching
M – measurable, meaningful, motivational
A – agreed upon, attainable, achievable, acceptable, action-oriented
R – realistic, relevant, reasonable, rewarding, results-oriented
T – time-based, time-bound, timely, tangible, trackable.

10 SMART *agile* objectives

1 **Fit-for-purpose products.** Starting with an MVP and building on it incrementally lets customers see the emerging product and tweak it where necessary. Thus converging on the best possible outcome and delivering a product that really does the business.

2 **Faster time to market.** No more endless waiting for a product that's past its sell-by date before it even arrives. The MVP gets a working product out of the door faster with add-ons following thick and fast.

3 **An early return on investment (ROI).** A base product is delivered quickly and enables benefits to be realised early on as the product continues to develop. The return starts sooner and builds from there. This achieves a much quicker ROI.

4 **Flexibility.** The one thing that's certain in life is change. Instead of putting on the change control manacles and swimming against the tide, *agile* embraces change and even encourages it. This is much better aligned with the natural way of (business) life.

5 **Less risk.** Starting smaller and building from there reduces the risk of outright failure enormously. On the rare occasions

that things do go a bit pear shaped, they can be fixed at a reasonable cost. Even minor disasters happen quickly and inexpensively.

6 **High visibility.** *Agile* provides excellent visibility for key stakeholders regarding both progress and the emerging product itself. Continuous involvement and collaboration means no more project silos or no-go areas.

7 **Greater efficiency.** Continuous improvement is a key part of a reflective *agile* culture. Widely publicised metrics are used to measure performance and teams are continually on the lookout for ways to do things. *Faster, cheaper, better* is the mantra but not at the expense of the quality of deliveries.

8 **Predictability.** A successful outcome is pretty much guaranteed: the business will get what it wants. Positive results are realised in the short term and this promotes a winning attitude. Success breeds confidence and leads to even more success, thus creating a virtuous circle.

9 **Satisfied customers.** Whatever criteria is applied to analysing customer satisfaction, expect tangible improvements early on. All and everything *agile* should make this a total no-brainer so be wary if the feedback is anything less than glowing. This is the ultimate litmus test.

10 **Better culture and morale.** Last but certainly not least, the end result of this is happy bunnies all round. A happy vibe in the business and self-satisfied grins in the project teams. This leads to a happier workforce and a winning culture where successful projects, not failures, are the norm.

Influencing the influencers

Even if existing projects are ramshackle affairs with no processes in place and total chaos reigns, there's currently no government

legislature that insists on fixing the problem using *agile*. In most environments things aren't awful, just pretty bad and *agile* will need a little help to get that first important chance to prove what can be done. Sometimes getting an initial opportunity is no big deal especially in smaller, flexible organisations but generally it's no shoo-in.

It's essential to get key influencers onside to create the first opening. There's no need to push for a full-scale rollout, as it's more *agile* to start small with a pilot project. The very essence of *agile* is to identify the MVP and build incrementally, and in that context one project is more than enough. Even if an offer is made to go for a big bang approach – and that does happen – starting small initially and then ramping up is a more effective way to build momentum.

It might even be well within your own gift to decide how the next project is run. If so, job done. Normally there's more to it than that but quite often it's down to just one person giving the thumbs-up. Perhaps the person responsible for dishing out projects needs to be convinced: maybe a formal programme

brilliant tip

There are only three *critical success factors* that are absolutely essential for an *agile* project launch:

1   the thumbs up for one suitable project;
2   business buy-in to providing active involvement;
3   access to keen people with an *agile* mind-set.

manager with multiple projects regularly on the go. Even in larger, heavily structured environments there will be someone with enough influence to make a pitch to. If all else fails, take a gamble and knock on the door of the CEO or the nearest accessible senior manager.

Even if it means going to the top, the message is unchanged and it will only take a matter of minutes to get it across. Armed with our *10 SMART agile objectives* to outline what can be achieved and a suitable project to recommend starting with, the chance of getting approval is very high.

Four sure-fire ways to get off on the wrong foot

✔ Proclaim *agile* as the only answer – either join the gang or hit the highway.

✔ Announce that it's all obvious – any idiot can pick it up, so no training is required.

✔ Declare *agile* is infallible – failures will be solely down to personal inadequacies.

✔ Dictate unreasonable targets and deadlines – explain that nothing is impossible in this brave new world.

Agile PR

Even before any pitch is made, the chances are that positive word-of-mouth will be helping out. Nearly everyone has heard something about the *agile* revolution and the advance press is consistently good. The movement isn't new but recent years have seen an explosion of interest and this is effectively the honeymoon period where everything in the garden is rosy. In fact, suggesting *agile* is anything less than perfect is considered heresy in some circles.

There's an amazing unofficial agile PR machine out there working to help and plenty of good news to tap into. There are stacks of high-profile organisations that believe passionately in the benefits of agile so why not pick out a few to name drop? Intel? Spotify? Google? How about good old Waitrose? These days it's getting hard to uncover organisations that aren't interested in leaping onto the bandwagon rather than the other way round. Any move made towards an *agile* environment is being made in very good company.

Pitching for piloting *agile* on a new project is going to be treated with respect. There might be a degree of doubt about whether *agile* can actually deliver on all the promises, but no one in their right mind is going to pooh-pooh what's on offer and if they do perhaps it's time to be looking for another job! The most likely outcome is the go-ahead for a pilot scheme and at worst a request for more information to validate the claims. The chances of a total knockback are negligible.

And if things get desperate, why not drop in the ultimate *agile* sound bite: *faster, cheaper, better* deliveries. There's much more to be said to properly explain that claim but ultimately it's a great sound bite.

 'If you're trying to persuade people to do something, or buy something, it seems to me you should use their language, the language they use every day, the language in which they think.'

David Ogilvy

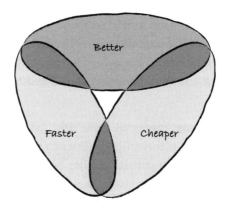

Not only for IT

One of the most popular misconceptions is that *agile* is only suitable for information technology (IT) projects. This is miles from the truth and most of the admired frameworks are suitable for anything. One of the key exceptions is Extreme Programming (XP) and the name itself is a bit of a giveaway. The automobile industry is way ahead of the curve with their close Lean tie-ins, and history shows IT to be a relatively late adopter. There's no doubt that a huge number of IT teams have embraced *agile* recently and they lay a fair claim to sparking the recent meteoric rise but this doesn't mean they have exclusive rights.

There's a widely held view that some departments within organisations are less likely to embrace *agile* with open arms but that's a long way from saying they're *absolutely* not suitable. Finance is one often-touted example of a reluctant suitor but even there the pickup is good if you search hard enough for examples. In fact it can be argued that *agile* projects can't function without an *agile* approach to the financial aspects and there's no point trying to launch an *agile* project with a fixed budget, fixed deliverables, a fixed timescale and no flexibility.

Of course there's no need to start the *agile* journey by picking on the toughest nuts to crack! IT projects aren't the only option but they're one of the best places to start looking.

▶ brilliant example

Before any project can be considered good to go, fundamental cultural prerequisites must be in place round the project to ensure *agile* principles and thinking can flourish. Without an *agile atmosphere*, the project will either wither and die or revert to old ways:

- **acceptance of the agile philosophy before starting** – including timeboxing, collaboration and iterative development;
- **decision-making powers within the team** – acceptance of empowerment;
- **commitment to provide significant business involvement** – guaranteed availability of the right resources;
- **agreement to incremental delivery** – acceptance that this is desirable and practical;
- **easy access to all team members** – preferably co-located teams or at least great comms facilities;

- **stability within the team** – commitment to a constant core team for the duration of the project;
- **correct skills and mind-sets** – a proficient team with good communication skills and tuned into agile;
- **size limits** –a small team to ensure good collaboration and communications;
- **supportive commercial arrangements** – trust and collaboration over contractual fine print.

This isn't about paying lip service to *agile* ways. It's easy enough to agree *in principle* with the *agile* ethos but putting those ideas into practice can be a quantum leap. For example, it's no use the business putting forward a junior gofer as a representative and then second-guessing every decision. Nor is there any point in empowering the team but expecting their decisions to be validated by a senior manager. To be successful it's necessary for everyone involved to walk the walk and talk the talk.

Measuring success

Metrics usually generate a pretty negative vibe. There was a time when the mere mention conjured up a mental image of a po-faced individual with a clipboard doing a time-and-motion study. Devotees have long argued that *if you can't measure something, it can't be improved* but it has proven near impossible to win people over. The bottom line was that metrics were always seen as management tool for squeezing more and more out of their workers.

Agile revolutionised the implementation of metrics and turned the whole thing on its head. Metrics are owned by the team and used by them to get the job done. Because of this shift of emphasis, metrics are better embraced as teams can now see exactly *what's in it for them*. Without these measurements,

 **definition**

The 1-2-3 for building performance metrics is:

- establish critical processes or customer requirements;
- identify specific, quantifiable outputs of work;
- establish targets against which results can be scored.

The metrics mantra is: measure, inspect and improve. Without measurement nothing else can follow.

agile – especially Scrum and Kanban – can't function properly. *Agile* metrics are still hugely useful to the wider organisation but they're no longer seen as a tool for controlling and squeezing more out of the workforce.

The team ownership of these metrics means they're much more reliable and that is a big selling point in the organisations. This is particularly apparent when measuring *velocity* (the output of an *agile* team), where the team calculate their speed of delivery and use that information to predict what they can deliver within given time constraints. The forecast is much more reliable because it's based on past experience. They're happy the targets aren't imposed or arbitrary and the business knows in advance exactly what they're going to get for their money.

Because *agile* is focused on delivering *business value*, the metrics are always couched in terms that the stakeholders can easily understand. The calculation process is executed internally and velocity is team specific but the eventual output is very precise. This subjective, team specific value can be used to calculate what the same bunch can deliver next time: for example, '*Agile* Team A will deliver features A, B and C after X weeks.' The business knows exactly what the team costs for that period of time and it's very clear what bang they're getting for their bucks.

 **example**

A quick start guide to using *agile velocity*:

- Agree a 1–5 scale that describes the relative size of work in ascending sequence (e.g. 1 = small, 5 = large).
- Assign a value to everything to be done by the team within a given timescale (e.g. two weeks).
- At the end, calculate the total number of units delivered – known as the team velocity.
- Track the minimum and maximum values to give the velocity range for the team.
- Ignore the highest and lowest values and average the others (total units delivered/total number of periods).
- Plan future work based on the average velocity.

Repeat the process until the planned and delivered velocities are consistent. Use this to predict what the business gets next.

Dual purpose reporting

Poor communication is usually cited as one of the biggest contributors when projects go off track. There's always been a tendency for traditional project managers to be over-optimistic at the start of any venture and then play down any bad news *en route* until it's far too late. This creates an uncertainty about the real state of play and sometimes a sense of foreboding from the very kick-off. This is a bad situation that isn't helped when the only feedback regarding progress is via irregular, indecipherable reports.

Once again, within an *agile* environment the set-up is totally different and turned on its head. The business team doesn't need to keep asking about progress because they're fully engaged and involved. Instead of spending time trying to pin down progress, the business team can concentrate on the right things. Time is spent instead on more productive activities.

Even though the right people will know exactly what the status of their project is because of their involvement, it's still vital to keep the rest of the organisation up to speed. This is in sharp contrast to the more traditional project reporting – such as the RAG status – that usually only makes sense to people in the know. An *agile* team is expected to publicise the fruits of their labour in the form of the delivered tangible business value and reliable predictions about the future.

 **definition**

Progress reports often use the traffic light rating system or *RAG status* definition as a visual cue to summarise performance for the benefit of stakeholders:

RED – significant issues blocking progress.

AMBER – obstructions that are being managed.

GREEN – everything is OK.

Agile project reporting is all about regular news and the updates can be expected every couple of weeks. This is totally focused on what has been delivered or what is scheduled for delivery soon – real news that the organisation can understand, with no place for sidetracking into excuses and cover-ups.

brilliant example

A useful tool for summarising progress is the project *burn up chart*. It tracks progress towards a project's completion, and in the most popular incarnation there are two lines on the chart:

1 total work – the project scope – over time;

2 accumulated work completed over time.

This is very different to the *sprint burn down*. It plots estimated total work in a project (frequently in story points) against the delivered work over time ▶

(usually story points within sprints). It tells a visual story of the project in progress by tracking deliveries against the total work required.

In the example below, the dashed line shows the total amount of story points in the project that the team needs to complete for a small proof of concept delivery that was meant to be short, concise and time-boxed to a maximum of eight one-week sprints. The dotted line is the accumulated total of story points the team has delivered.

After a slightly shaky start the development team starts to achieve a steady velocity but the Product Owner has regularly adjusted the requirements for them to work on. The conclusion is that the project will complete bang on time but not if even more requirements are added in the last two weeks.

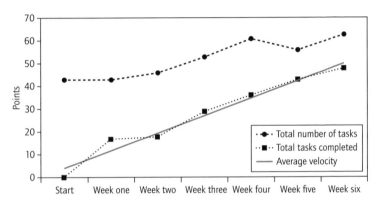

Figure 7.1 Brilliant burn up

Avoid repeating mistakes

Finally, *agile* doesn't offer total protection from typical tripwires, so be open-minded and learn from the hard-won experience of everyone whether *agile* or not. There's a tendency to be dismissive of the old school in some circles but there's much to be gleaned, especially regarding their most common *faux pas*. Fortunately many well-known lessons are already counteracted by

brilliant tip

Traditional tripwires can manifest themselves in the world of *agile* too. Don't let age-old problems re-emerge in the brave new world. There is nothing more damaging than the organisation thinking: *here we go again*. Forewarned is forearmed!

✗ **Unclear goals and objectives** – start with a clear *vision*.

✗ **Poorly defined business requirements** – get the *user stories* into great shape.

✗ **Inadequate training** – provide adequate training and coaching.

✗ **Unrealistic targets** – even *agile* can't meet impossible, externally imposed deadlines.

✗ **Over-committed resources** – let the team decide what they can realistically achieve.

✗ **Repeating mistakes** – the cardinal sin of any project framework; so always *inspect and adapt.*

the *agile* philosophy itself but don't be fooled into thinking *agile* provides an impregnable shield.

In the heat of the battle to get *agile* accepted it's important to remain realistic when making guarantees about *what* and *when*. Don't get carried away with the *faster, cheaper, better* message and promise the earth. Be especially careful not to be overly optimistic about the benefits of introducing *agile* and therefore over-egg the immediate upside. Don't commit to *brilliant* outcomes when *very good* is more than enough. A score of 9 out of 10 can be a bit disappointing when the expectation is a perfect score.

Be wary of people who may not understand all the ins and outs of *agile* working or perhaps have selective hearing. For a CEO it's tempting to stop listening after hearing the _big picture_ message of _faster, cheaper, better_. Or to only tune in for the promises of fit-for-purpose products, faster time to market, an early ROI, flexibility, less risk, high visibility, greater efficiency, predictability, satisfied customers with improved culture and morale thrown in to boot. Don't assume everyone pays attention to the small print and reads the terms and conditions, which of course they never do.

 'No one can whistle a symphony. It takes a whole orchestra to play it.'

H.E. Luccock

The final word

Ordinarily, projects find it very easy to operate in a silo and at times it even seems to be the accepted norm. Those projects are too often detached from the real world and what's really needed. The _agile_ way is very different of course and is built on a foundation of involvement and collaboration. The _minimum_ requirement is for specific business involvement in the project itself but wider organisational buy-in really helps, especially if the ultimate ambition is to use _agile_ as the _de facto_ standard for running projects.

Agile projects are by definition high profile as visibility and transparency are key objectives. It certainly helps if the _agile_ ethos and process is understood by everyone involved in touch points along the way including the likes of Finance and Marketing – both of whom are regularly ignored within a more traditional set-up. It pays dividends to publicise the basics of how _agile_ works and you can expect high levels of interest thanks to the excellent advance word-of-mouth. Don't be surprised to find the CEO, the Head of Finance and the equivalent from the Marketing department at any promo event. In fact, be disappointed if they're not.

There's no need to try and get everyone onside, as this isn't a crusade. But don't make the mistake of only paying attention to obvious candidates.

brilliant recap

- Get familiar with the business reasons for wanting to go *agile* and be prepared to talk in business terms to key decision makers.
- *Agile* is more than just an IT thing; aim to win over the whole organisation including the so-called *backwaters*.
- Reporting focused on deliverables and *real* progress is what the people want.
- Even the *old school* can help with learning lessons; they've made all the big mistakes many times before.
- Don't over-commit; even *brilliant* results can be a disappointment if you're expecting everything to be perfect.

CHAPTER 8

Support mechanisms

Introduction

One of the biggest selling points of *agile* is the unparalleled levels of support available, much of it completely *free*. The sense of community and belonging is quite astounding and it's always easy to find a helping hand. As always, the web is full of useful information and the only difficulty is in knowing where to start. There is extensive coverage of every possible relevant nuance and it's hard to find a stone unturned – even *agile* weight loss and *agile* mountaineering. The internet coverage of *PRINCE2* is stark in comparison.

That's not all. There's a choice of world class *non-profit making* support organisations with more training options on offer than anyone could possibly want in a professional lifetime. There are forums in the most unusual places and coverage in every possible aspect of modern media including webinars and Twitter. With more *agile* YouTube videos than *PRINCE2* and *The Muppet Show* combined. There's even a plentiful choice of excellent books!

Of course not everyone has altruistic motives. There are a few organisations with questionable credentials and the occasional outright pretender but nothing sinister. *Agilists* may come over as overly zealous sometimes but this isn't a worldwide religious cult. And there are plenty of people focused on making their living out of *agile*, of course, so expect to come across people with ulterior motives from time to time. If you post a question on an online forum asking for training recommendations then don't expect all of the advice to be independent.

The world of *agile* is one of fantastic choice and it only takes a minimal amount of research to find a good deal whatever you're looking for. If the budget's really tight it's possible to get started for next to nothing.

 'A true teacher will never guide you through the door, only to the door.'

Nikki Rowe

Getting started

Being spoilt for choice is a double-edged sword. Whatever you're looking for, however obscure or mainstream, it's out there. The $64,000 question is: what's the best thing to do next after reading this book? Well, that's a mighty fine question and not one that's easy to answer but if we're going to come off the fence then the answer is: check out LinkedIn groups.

These days all professionals are expected to have a LinkedIn account and with close to 400 million members worldwide in 2015 we're going to take a small punt and assume you know all about this global phenomenon (if not then set up a free account straight away at **www.linkedin.com** and discover the professional social networking version of Facebook without the silver surfers and pictures of babies).

There are more agile-centric groups on LinkedIn than you've had hot dinners and all of the main ones are open and welcoming to all, especially inquisitive novices. Or join one of the mainstream project management groups for a more across the board view. Even better join one of each. Our personal favourites are Scrum Practitioners and the Project Managers Network.

No *agile* stone is left unturned in the former and get ready to witness the passion of discussions however light the subject. Don't be afraid to post a question – these are the most inclusive and forgiving boards in town – but always apply the normal common sense filters. Asking for training recommendations, for example, will generate good advice but the vultures will start circling too.

LinkedIn is a great toe-dipper and a zero-cost entry into the wild and wonderful world of *agile*.

 **example**

One innocent newbie posted a question on a popular LinkedIn Scrum group about whether it was OK to take notes during the daily stand up meeting and circulate them afterwards as an *aide-mémoire*. A pretty straightforward question at first glance.

Apart from a few *yeah, go ahead* type responses, there was a lengthy, in-depth examination of the reasons and motives behind wanting to take notes. Was there an ulterior *command-and-control* motive behind sending out directive notes after the meeting? Was this highlighting a fundamental problem with the daily stand up itself or even with the whole Scrum set-up?

Even if you ask a seemingly simple question, no agile stone is left unturned.

Support organisations and other communities

The Agile Alliance is one of the biggies out there, some would argue the biggest and the best. In their own words they're a non-profit organisation with global membership, committed to advancing *agile* development principles and practices. At around $100 for an ordinary individual and less than double that for a corporate membership for up to five people, this provides amazing value for the resources on tap. Looks good on your CV too!

As the names suggests, the Scrum Alliance and Scrum.org are, not surprisingly, Scrum-centric but are open to discuss mainstream *agile* topics too. Both offer membership as part of their certification package and a basic membership too. Once again, the extensive resources available on tap are a big draw and there's a huge sense of community. There are probably completists who are members of both but usually one or the other is more than enough.

Another great destination for anyone interested in *agile* is Yahoo Groups where almost every nuance seems to be covered. So if you're a Spanish speaking *agile* software development practitioner or more interested in Lean or Kanban there's bound to be something of interest. The problem can be in finding the right niche but nothing that a little digging can't sort out.

Then finally there are the usual highly respected project management communities that, of course, recognise the *agile* phenomenon. The Association for Project Management and the Project Management Institute are considered highly respected sources by project managers and well worth checking out. The list goes on and on, enough to say that the choice is close to endless.

Conferences

Agile conferences are a bit like music festivals these days. There's always a local event nearby and if travelling further afield is an option, the world is your oyster. *Agile* conferences are not geared up for experts only and reading this book is more than enough of a primer before going to one. There are generic events about *agile* but many focus on specialisms or frameworks. Lean and Six Sigma, Kanban, Scrum, product management and testing are part of an enormous list

So far we've not come across one catering for *agile* heavy metal fans but there is something for pretty much every other taste. A good example of what's on offer is *Agile On The Beach* (check out **www. agileonthebeach.com**). It's big enough to be comprehensive, small enough to be intimate. Fine for beginners but plenty of specialist material and a damn fine location. Check out their conference videos on YouTube for a sneak preview – links are on their website – plenty of material for novices and experts too. This is our favourite type of *agile* event in terms of bang for your bucks.

At the other extreme there are much bigger set pieces including the Glastonbury-esque Agile Alliance Conference in the US. Our experience is that there are enough great local shows to avoid transatlantic travel but there's no doubting that international *agile* conferencing is big business too. The opportunities for networking at any big gun event are phenomenal and the organisation is normally much slicker with more chance of hanging out with the *agile* glitterati too. There's something out there for everyone.

Don't forget that all the decent conferences publish their material, so our advice is: try before you buy. It's sensible to get a feel for a conference before attending.

Agile conference tips

The people who attend a conference are normally more important than material on offer. Without doubt the best IT conference in the world is the annual QA&TEST event in Bilbao, Spain (see **www.qatest.org** for details). The organisers are just lovely, ditto their supporting committee and they attract a great crowd from all over the world. The location is brilliant and the attention to detail is second to none. The event specialises in software quality assurance and testing on embedded systems – quite a mouthful – but the big selling point is the diverse nature of the attendees, somewhat surprising given the event theme. As a bonus, many of the unsung *agile* elite end up there as conference speakers.

Read between the lines of the programme of events and check out the word of mouth.

Connecting up with others

Sitting at home, surfing the web and checking out the forums is a bit impersonal and has serious limitations. It's obviously a bit anti-social and feels a bit anti-*agile* too – the whole *agile* ethos is based on interaction with others. Conferences usually require a considerable investment of time (and sometimes money too), so a local *soirée* is a good alternative. There was a time when a gathering of *experts* was a dour event and no self-respecting *bon vivant* would consider attending. Things are different these days.

All the usual suspects host regular events and that's one of the side benefits of signing up with an *agile* organisation; these are pretty good on the whole. Certainly it's a no-brainer if you've joined up anyway but not always a reason for taking out membership in its own right. Another option is to find a local group using **www.meetup.com** or by asking around. There are groups all over the country and don't be too worried if there appears to be a specialist slant like Kanban, Scrum or Lean. People who attend *agile* gatherings are invariably open-minded.

Meet-ups tend to be smaller, more informal and provide a great opportunity to get a meaningful conversation going with a local practitioner or expert. The larger ones are great for exposure to bigger organisations, great case studies and internationally known personalities. Be aware that just because someone is on a stage or highly vocal at a gathering doesn't mean the material delivered is rock solid. Don't forget many people have ulterior motives and some even pay to speak! So keep an eye out for glorified sales pitches.

As an aside, don't get **www.meetup.com** confused with the dating website www.meet.com. Specifying an interest in *agile* there will lead to unpredictable results.

Get prepared

Because of the ease of entry to the world of *agile*, it is tempting to read a couple of articles and then get stuck in. There's nothing wrong with a can-do approach and there's no substitute for learning on the job – especially where *agile* is concerned. If common sense and due diligence are applied, it's easy enough to get up to a reasonable level of competence quickly, painlessly and for next to nothing. All this comes with a caveat: don't be tempted to assume that because *agile* is easy to understand that it's easy to get right.

The core concept behind this book is to give each reader enough to get going: our equivalent of the *minimum viable product*. There's nothing wrong with building on that foundation and in the medium term that makes plenty of sense. There are zero-risk, zero-cost options for supplementing the material here: for example, the excellent material out at **www.scrumtrainingseries.com**. For most, this book plus the video training there is more than enough food for thought. The coverage for *agile* generally and

Scrum is half-decent on YouTube and just about worth checking out. Something for nothing as they say.

When it comes to formal training it really becomes a minefield. There are good courses covering *agile* generally and every possible nuance. The expression *spoilt for choice* springs to mind. This is one area where there's no definitive right answer but it's always worth going on one with a decent track record that is peppered with practical hands-on exercises. Sitting around for two days listening to a trainer talk, talk, talk is of limited benefit. The final litmus test we recommend is simply: does it do the job *and* is it CV enhancing?

The problem with all standard training is that it's usually knowledge based so there's only so much that can be achieved in two to five days. It's great for mass inductions to the world of Scrum but for an individual there are other equally viable options. On balance it's worth doing but more for appearances than anything else.

brilliant tip

There's a mistaken belief that in the world of *agile* nothing gets written down. That was the case with many ancient civilisations and with the modern day Mafia but it's an urban myth when it comes to *agile*.

Go onto Amazon books and search on 'agile'. An extensive choice and the majority were published in the last couple of years.

Formal training options

Agile training comes in a different shapes and sizes but all options have similar benefits, namely getting people to speak about *agile* in a common language while trying out a few techniques in a safe learning environment. It is impossible to recommend specific courses because of the huge number of different combinations – so much depends on the nuances of needs. But there are two main factors to consider:

1 **Certified or non-certified.** Certified training gets you a *qualification* and non-certified doesn't. Certified training tends to be more expensive and less flexible regarding content – you just follow the syllabus. Non-certified courses are often tailored to specific needs, are on the whole cheaper and of course don't leave you with anything formal. Certified tends to look better on the CV but there are better non-certified courses available if you look hard enough.

brilliant tip

Not everyone is convinced by the mass-market certification game and the question is often asked: *who certifies the people that certify the certificate givers anyway?*

Consider a non-certified course and consider using the money saved for a night out.

2 **Public or private.** A private course is one that is done in-house for an organisation; many focus on helping specific teams. These are privately negotiated and can be certified but tend to be used for tailored, non-certified material. A public course is a scheduled event, commonly held at a training venue and anyone can book onto it. These courses tend to have a much wider appeal but don't focus on the specifics of a company, project or product as the group will invariably be from a diverse professional background. The best public courses are a great networking opportunity; meeting other people with similar interests and similar circumstances is illuminating and a taster of the advantages of joining an *agile* community.

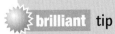 **tip**

Looking for certified *agile* training is like pogo-sticking through a minefield. Accredited courses are much of a muchness in terms of content but some trainers know their onions and some just know the course material. As with everything, recommendations make a big difference here. And naming no names, there are members of the *agile* glitterati that offer training if star tracking floats your boat.

Coaching and mentoring

We may have mixed emotions about some aspects of formal training but the same isn't true about coaching and mentoring. Getting in an experienced coach to help and guide an *agile* team has a positive impact from day one. The best coaches come in and hit the ground running. More often than not teams need help with the mechanics of *agile* and questions are very specific. Coaches help to fine-tune in those situations. But if the issues are more fundamental, they're experienced in going back to basics and laying down strong foundations.

An *agile* coaching role isn't normally a full-time job even if money is no object. There's always a risk of creating team dependency if guidance is on tap and far better to restrict this to one or two days per week. Little and often works well in most organisations. If there are good reasons to get someone in full-time it's a better option to give them some *real work* as well to do, and therefore lead by example.

If *agile* is launched *en masse* throughout an organisation, getting in a coach will increase the likelihood of success considerably. Don't get hung up on the cost of getting in a coach, think about the cost of *not* getting one in. If in any doubt, see what can be achieved in a couple of days spread over a month. Expect to see the team improving individually and collectively. And expect to see tangible results in terms of productivity straight away; the bottom line is that this mentoring will be self-financing.

Getting the best out of a coach from an individual perspective is easy. For a start, they're measured by *your success* not your opinions. *Agile* coaching is a bit like personal counselling; *agile* coaches aren't there to judge, only to guide. Their advice helps make tweaks that can be the difference between success and failure. For example, a dysfunctional daily stand up is so much easier to turn around with the guidance of a seasoned pro.

If an independent coach isn't a viable option, the preferred alternative is to seek out other experienced support within the organisation and build an internal *agile* community. *Agilists* are naturally supportive, and looking for help is deemed a positive move, not a cry for help. And if all else fails, look for virtual support on *agile* forums or within communities. Even the *dumbest* questions get answered sympathetically and some of them ain't as stupid as they appear!

brilliant tip

Try relaxing with an on-topic film:

● *Titanic* – a big budget project hits the rocks, literally.

● *Groundhog Day* – learning lessons the hard way.

● *Psycho* – not everyone has an *agile* mind-set.

● *Downfall* – the ultimate consequence of command and control.

● *12 Angry Men* – top consensus reaching and influencing.

● *Kung-Fu Panda* – great teams are sometimes the unlikely ones.

Podcasts and webinars

Podcasts and webinars sum up one of the key problems with the modern tech age. There's no doubt about the volume of material out there, the question mark is against the quality. There are a few decent podcasts and webinars but it's painful seeking them out. There are too many marketing campaigns and products teasers in disguise and there are far too many frogs that need kissing before you meet a dreamboat.

There are some signs this is changing and there are a few individual jewels but on the whole it's better to give these products a swerve. We look forward to being innundated with rebuttals and great examples in this fast-changing market!

'Successful people are always looking for opportunities to help others. Unsuccessful people are always asking, "What's in it for me?"'

Brian Tracy

The final word

The *agile* community is built on sharing, collaboration and trust. In terms of support there's no other professional association that comes close. The *agile* mind-set is sympathetic, helpful and protective of their own gang – great news if help is needed and woe betide anyone who wants to muscle in to take advantage or make quick bucks. The community rounds on charlatans and cheats in the blink of an eye.

The sheer volume of material available is a problem, so the key is in being selective. Many of the forums are self-regulating in that respect, as people vote with their feet and the poor ones quickly wither and die. It doesn't take much effort to seek out the best ones. It's a similar situation with the other support on offer.

The breath and quality of support is astounding but there's good and bad out there. *Caveat emptor.*

This can all be a bit of a minefield but this navigation is part of the *agile* journey. Working out the difference between great advice and a personal opinion is all part of getting into the groove. In terms of support mechanisms this is a golden age for anyone thinking of taking the plunge or is already in the space.

Don't pinch us in case we wake up.

 **recap**

- There's a wealth of free information out there so fill your boots; at least head over to LinkedIn.

- All that glitters isn't gold; don't blindly accept everything you hear and instead form your own opinions.

- Formal training is CV enhancing but there are better options available if only results matter.

- Mentoring and coaching don't come free but they usually pay for themselves.

- Seek out new information and ideas but, above all, *remain true to thyself.*

CHAPTER 9

A call to action

Introduction

There's a good chance that the motivation for reading this book is much more than just a passing interest in *agile* theory or curiosity about all of the hullabaloo. Perhaps there's a new *agile* role in the offing or maybe an opportunity looming to run a project *differently*? Whatever the backdrop, pure research into *agile* has its limitations and thinking about going *agile* isn't enough. The best way to learn about it *properly* is to roll up your sleeves and get started.

One of the key things to keep in mind is that *agile* is a mind-set more than anything else. It's about thinking differently and approaching traditional problems in new ways. Processes can be severely constraining and *agile* aims to be *liberating* by encouraging us to adapt to change quickly and inventively. The idea of *inspect and adapt* is at the heart of the *agile* ethos, not a series of set rules and regulations.

Agile thinking is unique because it can be applied to *any* situation. That might be a personal one like planning a wedding or moving house and *personal* Kanban can be a fun place to start. It may be for running projects within a business or charity or even for jobs within specific disciplines like marketing or sales. Whatever the reason, there really isn't anywhere that *agile* doesn't work because it's a set of guiding principles that are used to make things better by empowering people, removing waste and improving quality.

So after a long haul and some pretty dark days, the future is much brighter for projects and the people working on them. Yes the future is looking good; the future is going to be far more *agile*. Let's get on with the job. Let's get into action.

 'As we look ahead into the next century, leaders will be those who empower others.'

Bill Gates

Enabling agility

The people who are best at getting *agile* to work have an open mind about how to achieve clear goals. They know the outcome that's wanted and are scientific yet flexible in their approach to getting there. Always trying new things, just a few at a time and then keeping what works and dropping the stuff that doesn't. Those with an *agile* mind-set don't beat themselves up when things go wrong but pick themselves up, dust themselves off and try another idea in search of a *better way*.

These natural *agile* practitioners also know a simple fact: it's all about people, *not* processes or technology. If the focus is on getting the right people working effectively together to achieve well-defined goals, then success is sure to follow. *Agile* enables this to happen and, after all, what's the point of getting a great team of experts together and then driving them into the ground with restrictive processes, arbitrary management targets and other false constraints?

To get the best out of people who are trying to solve a problem, there are a few simple yet fundamental things that need to happen:

- **Define a clear vision.** Fix the target and describe the outcomes unmistakably with a vision statement that is meaningful and has achievable acceptance criteria.

- **Agree the roles and responsibilities.** Get the required experts together and ensure everyone knows the part they'll play, so they can get on with the job effectively.

- **Remove any obstacles that get in the way.** Make it as simple for teams to deliver as it can be. Observe and then act.

> ### brilliant tip
>
> Starting an *agile* project is like going for a walk. Know where you're heading and then put one foot in front of the other one.
>
> *And be prepared to sidestep any obstacles on the way.*

Back to first principles

Whatever else happens, always stick to the *agile* first principles. Don't get hung up on the subtleties and intricacies of Scrum or Kanban; concentrate on adhering to the *Agile Manifesto* and the Lean thinking behind it. This guidance is easy to understand plus simple and cheap to implement yet just about sums it all up. Everything *agile* is built around these core ideas and any new concept, method or practice will share their DNA.

People seem to have a tendency to overcomplicate things. Over the years many have tried to re-brand, re-invent or re-proposition the core concepts into flashy, shiny, exquisitely packaged and generally expensive products, services or even *new* ideas. It's easy to be negative about this and say it's all about making money, but it's part of an evolution from very solid foundations. Just make sure the new ideas stack up against the original principles before investing time or money into them. And remember: if something sounds too good to be true, it probably is.

If at any point things start getting too complicated, you've missed something, somewhere along the way. If things go badly from time

to time, that's natural as occasional setbacks are to be expected. Getting started and then continually improving little by little is quite normal. Expect immediate results but not a quick fix.

Getting started

There's a golden rule with getting started with *agile*: *start simple*. Remember, the most basic *agile* process doesn't even require a framework like Scrum or Kanban. To get started, all that's needed is a set of requirements prioritised by value in a list. Start with the item at the top of the list first. Don't forget to keep an eye on the *Agile Manifesto* and there's plenty of best practice to tap into within the material covered here.

It's possible to pare down to the bare bones but we strongly recommend starting with either Kanban or Scrum. These frameworks are fantastic tools to help get going, providing a set of guidelines that are proven to work and a support community ready and willing to offer *free* help and advice. Even the best frameworks are slightly constraining if used rigidly, so think about their strengths and weaknesses then try them out with an open mind. Once in play, *inspect and adapt* to get things purring.

Avoid layering anything in without good reason. Don't add processes for the sake of show or because someone else said it was a good idea. Add process because it's needed to help deliver quality products or services.

brilliant dos and don'ts

Based on experience, there are *dos and don'ts* for taking the first step:

Do . . .
- ✔ Pick a small, low-risk problem or project to try out *agile*.
- ✔ Explain to people why you think it will be useful.
- ✔ Have a clear vision, goals or objectives.
- ✔ Make what you do transparent and visible.
- ✔ Get started as soon as you can.

Don't . . .
- ✘ Do it on your own.
- ✘ Get hung up on process.
- ✘ Take too much on.
- ✘ Try too many new things at once.
- ✘ Overcomplicate it.

Continuous improvement

Learning from setbacks and bouncing back quickly is what *agile* is all about. How many times have you thought to yourself: *if only I'd known then what I know now*? There's no doubting the power of learning lessons – both things to do differently given the chance and bright ideas that worked out well – and *agile* bakes this into the heart of process. From the very early Lean days, it was accepted that there's room for improvement in everything we do, and an open-minded approach to process improvement pays dividends.

In many respects this encapsulates the difference between *agile* and more traditional approaches to project management. *Agile* encourages close scrutiny and sees learning from lessons as a positive thing, not an embarrassing problem. Weaknesses are turned into strengths. Instead of trying to cover tracks or launch a witch-hunt for a suitable scapegoat, learning lessons is treated as a natural part of the process. There's no need to make all the mistakes yourselves; aim to tap into the collective experience of others.

Just as change is embraced by *agile*, mistakes are acted on in a positive way too and are never considered to be the end of the world. Good practice is encouraged and built on as well. The *agile* ethos is to be continually in search of process improvements.

---

brilliant example

Thomas Edison tried 2,000 different materials in search of a filament for the light bulb. When none worked satisfactorily, his assistant complained, 'All our work is in vain. We have learned nothing.' Edison replied very confidently, 'Oh, we have come a long way and we have learned a lot. We know that there are 2,000 elements which we cannot use to make a good light bulb.'

A tale from the dark ages. Literally.

Always learning

Learning lessons is normally an unenthusiastic bolt-on just before closing time. There's usually a great deal of reluctance to look back and reflect so there are few complaints if it doesn't happen at all. When a *lessons learned* session does go ahead, it's often seen as an opportunity to settle long-running feuds. Fingers are pointed and accusations fly. Then finally to add insult to injury, results are seldom acted on and the recommendations are filed away in cyberspace, never to be seen again.

With Lean and Kanban, learning lessons and improving the assembly line is the *raison d'être*, not an optional extra. The initial driver was to fine-tune the production process and by definition that means recognising blips along the way. Because of the *agile* team culture nobody is singled out for criticism or praise and that builds an open and honest working environment. Mudslinging and personal attacks are considered very un-*agile*.

With Scrum, *retrospectives* as they're known are part of the furniture – one of the regular sprint ceremonies. Instead of waiting until it's all over, the lessons are learned at the end of each sprint and incorporated immediately. The team applies their collective knowledge to early feedback and solves problems while they're small and easy to tackle, then stops them reoccurring. One of the strongest signs of a dysfunctional team is if this *isn't* happening.

Happier teams deliver better. Everyone prefers to work in a place where their frustrations are dealt with and their jobs are continually made easier. This breeds confidence and leads to success. It also creates a virtuous circle. Improving morale, environment, process, product, communication and so on encourages the team to search for *even more* improvements. Onwards and upwards!

The future for *agile*

One thing's for certain: *agile* is definitely not another flash in the pan. Over the years other wizardry has come and gone but this is the real deal. Much of it is common sense and the rest is very logical and easy to pick up. Many people who look into *agile* are surprised at the simplicity of it all. The recent take-up has been phenomenal and it shows no sign of abating. This is because it does what is says on the tin.

brilliant tip

There's no doubt that *agile* isn't just for small projects but scaling up does require extra care and attention. And there's a big difference between scaling up in terms of the amount of work in the backlog and working with multiple *agile* teams as part of a programme of connected work.

A bigger backlog isn't such a big problem and sometimes it's one of the consequences of success. The bigger issue is when the work gets too much for one team or more than one is needed from the outset. Running multiple, connected *agile* teams is another kettle of fish. At the very least, keep the conversations flowing between all of the teams.

Scrum offers a solution that can be applied anywhere. Teams are kept down to their optimum, manageable size and each team designates one member as an *ambassador* to participate in a daily meeting with ambassadors from the other teams; known as *the Scrum of Scrums*. This approach can be used whatever the framework.

So, where is *agile* going now? In some ways *agile* is becoming a victim of its own success. Many have already tried to constrain it with their own rules, regulations and even reputations. Some have tried to turn it into a commodity that can be sold, or even pseudo-trademark it by bolting on their own specialist intellectual property. This is picking up pace but there's no hard evidence of *agile* getting badly misrepresented or dragged away from its core roots and values.

Getting bigger and being adopted more widely comes with some significant problems. There are more opportunities for misuse and misunderstandings. For example, big corporations have tried to *go agile* because they think it means great results with minimal effort and found out the reality is very different. Others have given up after implementing *agile* badly and getting it dreadfully wrong but blame the tools not their tradespeople. There's no doubt that the honeymoon period is coming to an end and there's evidence of a critical backlash – never malicious but usually misinformed.

PRINCE2 has a more secure future because it is *owned* and tightly controlled. It hasn't changed much over the years and is unlikely to do so in the foreseeable future – it's safe, steady and reliable. In contrast nobody owns the *agile* trademark, there are just a number of guardians of the flame. Anything can happen with *agile* because everyone has a say. That makes it exciting but less unpredictable. Watch this space.

Figure 9.1 Agile umbrella

Remember the basics

Whatever happens down the line, don't lose sight of the guiding principles of *agile* and guard against going too far off-piste. Every so often take time out to go back to basics and spend time mulling over the *Agile Manifesto* and the principles behind it, Lean values, the *Declaration of Interdependence,* the *Scrum Guide* plus anything that is at the heart of *agile* thinking. Avoid getting obsessed with the day-to-day nuances but keep true to the spirit of it all. *Agile* is above everything else a mind-set:

- **Focus on tangible outputs.** Good practitioners obsess over delivering business value and benefit; it's everything. Having the courage to say when something isn't right, passionately trying to make the lives of users better and always keeping the business *vision* in mind is at the heart of it all.

- **Make what you do visible.** The best way to guarantee success is to help others see what's going on so they can chip in with their skills and experience. Hidden work doesn't get done. Problems that are concealed don't get addressed. The team can't help with things they know nothing about.

- **Share everything.** Without sharing there can be no *inspect and adapt*, there can be no continuous improvement. Sharing is also about listening, encouraging and developing, so don't knock back ideas out of hand. Sharing is the basis for learning.

- **Be cooperative and collaborative.** The power of *agile* is in the strength of a self-managing team working together with a common goal in focus. Being open and honest, being supportive and operating as a collective will guarantee success. You're only as good as the people around you.

brilliant example

Auditors wanted to scrutinise two projects as part of a general corporate health check. It was a mixed environment using *agile* and more traditional working practices. The auditors were particularly interested in the supporting documentation that was available.

The *agile* team were very candid. Documentation was pretty sparse and they'd stuck to the barebones, *must have* stuff. In contrast, the project manager took the auditors over to a cabinet filled with reams and reams of material. Afterwards, in private, the PM confessed to the *agile* team that none of it was ever used!

The audit came back with a glowing assessment for the wily old PM and a could-do-better rating for the *agile* team.

Sometimes you can't do right for doing wrong. Openness and honesty may backfire occasionally but it's always the best policy.

The final word

So this is the end of our journey together. *What next?* Well, doing nothing is always an option on any project whether personal or professional, so possibly this book and the whole *agile* thing will be put to one side and forgotten. However passionate we feel about the benefits of *agile*, we understand it's not for everyone. Dropping out may be down to insurmountable organisational blockers or maybe *agile* just doesn't hit the right spot. We acknowledge that *agile* isn't a panacea for all ills.

Hopefully there will be many more who want to continue the journey and get cracking for real – and even more who are already *en route*. Either way it's not going to be a cakewalk; *agile* frameworks are easy to understand and equally easy to get wrong. But armed with an open mind and support from the *agile* community, it's going to be fine. One option we use is to have a personal *backlog* of things to try out and bash through them one by one.

Kanban and Scrum are simply brilliant, but never get hung up on a framework, as it's always a means to an end not the meaning of life. Keep it simple and be open to change – that's something that will happen for sure. Try to set off with others, as at heart it's a team thing and operating in isolation doesn't work so well. Hook up with like-minded individuals in and outside work – it's more fun, and a diverse group of people lends different aspects of advice and fresh ideas. Build the excitement and learn together.

Fortunately *agile* has a very low barrier to entry. Some even start off without even knowing it! There's no need to be trained up, get certified or spend any money to get going. All you need to do is be brave enough to give it a go.

Good luck. Let us know how it all worked out.

 To improve is to change; to be perfect is to change often.

Winston Churchill

What did you think of this book?

We're really keen to hear from you about this book, so that we can make our publishing even better.

Please log on to the following website and leave us your feedback.

It will only take a few minutes and your thoughts are invaluable to us.

www.pearsoned.co.uk/bookfeedback

Index